AND HAVE NO FELLOWSHIP WITH THE UNFRUITFUL WORKS OF DARKNESS, BUT RATHER EXPOSE *THEM*.

EPHESIANS 5:11

WITHOUT PREJUDICE

INSIDE AN IRISH COURTROOM
AND THE ILLUSION OF FAIRNESS

PART ONE

Without Prejudice – Part One

First published in 2026.

Published by Eternal Legacy Publishing

Paperback edition:

ISBN 978-1-0668-4630-6

This book is a work of non-fiction based on the author's personal experiences, contemporaneous records, publicly available documents and research. Every effort has been made to ensure the accuracy of quotations, dates and references at the time of publication. Readers are encouraged to examine the source material and reach their own conclusions.

Book design and layout by David Morrissey

www.davemorrissey.ie

ETERNAL
LEGACY
PUBLISHING

Contents

DISCLAIMER

Nothing in this book is legal advice – don't even go there.

I am not a lawyer, I do not give legal advice, and nothing here should be relied upon as such. This book is not a how-to guide, a manual, or a shortcut through any legal process. Anyone who needs legal advice should seek it from someone properly qualified.

What follows is a first-person account of events as they unfolded before me. It is written from my perspective only, based on my direct involvement and contemporaneous records. Where opinions, impressions, or conclusions appear, they are personal opinions formed in good faith at the time, not assertions of objective fact.

Every effort has been made to describe events and documents accurately, but no claim is made that this account is exhaustive or infallible. The text reflects my understanding then and now; others may remember things differently.

Where courts, proceedings, correspondence, or regulators are discussed, they are referred to only by reference to publicly available materials and my own records. Individuals and institutions are named solely because they were directly involved. All references are made in good faith, without malice, and limited to what was raised, recorded, argued, or determined within the relevant proceedings or correspondence at the time.

Nothing in these pages should be taken as a statement of fact about any person or body unless clearly established by a public record cited in context.

Persons and organisations are named because they form part of the factual narrative. Omitting them would make the account incomplete or misleading. I have no intention of softening the account for the sake of diplomacy or appearances. The underlying records exist. Readers are, as always, encouraged to reach their own conclusions.

A note on supporting documents:

There is a mountain of paperwork behind this book: correspondence, affidavits, court filings, orders, transcripts, contemporaneous notes and assorted other records accumulated over many years. I have chosen not to reproduce all of it here for the simple reason that doing so would probably double the size of the book and bury the story beneath paperwork.

Where particular documents matter, they are referred to in context. The originals and supporting records remain in my possession and have been retained. Their absence from these pages should not be mistaken for their absence altogether.

Anyone who doubts the accuracy or veracity of what is described in this book should therefore understand that the account was not written from memory alone. Should any statement contained within these pages ever be formally challenged, the relevant underlying records can be produced immediately and relied upon as appropriate.

PROLOGUE

I had intended to release this book only when the story was finished.

That was the plan, anyway. Part One – the account of how I got into trouble when the crash of 2008 hit me (and thousands of others); how I was dragged through the courts and a possession order was granted against my home in 2017; how I fought my way through the High Court and even lodged documents with the Supreme Court; and how I eventually reached an exhausted armistice – has been sitting in a folder on my laptop for the better part of a year, waiting for Part Two to catch up.

Part Two was supposed to be the second half of the same book – the ending, whatever it turned out to be. I wanted to hand readers a complete saga, not a cliffhanger. I really did not want to release two books… just the one.

But the ending keeps moving.

As I write this, the case is back winding its way through Naas Circuit Court a second time. A new firm of solicitors has picked up where the old one left off, and a new plaintiff has been parachuted in. I am still fighting, still documenting, still coming up against the same ridiculous methodologies; the same ritualistic horse shit; and still waiting for the system to deliver whatever it considers to be justice. I'm not holding my breath on that last point – experience having told me not to expect any.

I could keep waiting. I could sit on Part One until the next hearing, or the one after that, or the appeal after that, or the LSRA determination after that, or whatever comes next. But I've been waiting for over a decade already, and I've learned that the Irish legal system does not operate on any timetable but its own.

So I'm releasing Part One now. Not because the whole story is over, but because one distinct part of it is.

What follows is a complete account of the years 2007 to 2021: the crash, the collapse, the courtroom education, and the various kicks in the nuts. It documents a system that rewards delay, punishes transparency, and treats self-represented litigants as an inconvenience to be managed and swatted away rather than actual people to be heard.

The events described in these pages have already been adjudicated. The possession order was granted. The attempts to appeal were slapped down before they could begin. That particular chapter is closed (for now).

What happened next – the resurrection of the case in 2025 without my knowledge, and what I was seeing as the return of some very familiar and dirty tactics – is Part Two. That story is still unfolding before me in real time. I'll release it when it reaches its own conclusion, whatever and whenever that may be. Ultimately, that release date is not up to me. It may be next year or five years from now.

In the meantime, this is where it began. The fight, as it turns out, is far from over.

I wish you well.

David Morrissey
July 2026

BEFORE WE BEGIN

Let's strip away a myth.

For generations we were conditioned to respect certain people automatically – priests, bankers, politicians, lawyers. They were society's "trusted classes," the ones we were meant to look up to. We now know where blind respect can lead: abused trust, hollowed-out institutions, and ordinary people left to carry the cost.

As trust in institutions has declined, more people have begun looking beyond official narratives. The public is seeing what many already suspected – those presented as guardians of morality and law are often the most skilled at navigating, bending and exploiting the very systems they operate within. Scratch the surface, and beneath the ritual and rhetoric you find the same appetites that drive every other bully: power, money, and freedom from consequence.

Take the legal class. If you've never needed a solicitor, you might still believe the marketing myth – the measured professional guided by truth and justice, speaking calmly on your behalf, integrity unquestioned. That illusion lasted about five minutes once I met the reality of a courtroom.

In the courtroom I came to know, the solicitor's mission seemed brutally simple: to win – by whatever means necessary. Not to find justice, and not even necessarily to tell the truth – just to win. From where

I stood, if the facts don't fit, they'll be stretched. If evidence threatens the case, it will be buried in "procedure" or possibly omitted entirely. If intimidation works, it will be used. They call it advocacy. From the other side of the room, it looks like strategy without limits, or scruples.

Here's the part most people never see: in an adversarial system, honesty is a liability. A solicitor who plays fair is already at a disadvantage. Courtroom "truth" becomes whatever survives objection in the few seconds before the next file is opened. The system rewards dexterity, not integrity.

I walked into Naas Circuit Court in April 2015 believing the courtroom was the last refuge of truth. It's amazing to me now that in my then mid-40s I *still* actually thought cases were decided by evidence, not tactics. By lunchtime on my very first day, I saw that it was a chessboard – and I was the only player who still thought the pieces stood for something more than points. The rest were professionals of persuasion, deflection, omission – good at it, paid for it, and utterly unashamed of it.

Yet for all the polish, one thing hasn't changed: bullies still falter when you push back with evidence and persistence. What they don't expect is for an ordinary person to learn the rules, quote those rules back accurately, and keep meticulous records. When that happens, confidence drains and the mask slips.

That's where this book begins. Not as a crusade against institutions, but as a record of what one ordinary person discovered when he stopped *backing* down and started *writing* down. There's no conspiracy theory here – just blunt experience – all of it backed by actual paperwork… or to use another word you may know: *evidence*. Those who still believe the system naturally favours truth may find this uncomfortable; those who've been through it will find it familiar.

So if you've ever wondered what really happens when you find yourself up against obscenely paid legal representatives, keep reading. Everything that follows happened in public courts, recorded by Judges, clerks, and Digital Audio Recording systems. The names are real; so are the consequences.

Before going any further, I should make one thing clear. This is not an attack on every solicitor. My experience is limited to those acting for banks and other lenders in possession proceedings. I have no doubt there are many solicitors of integrity. I even have some in my own extended family. Unfortunately, none of those I encountered during my own case gave me any reason to revise my opinion. This book is about those experiences and the documents that record them.

Welcome to the reality behind the myth.

Without Prejudice

Part One

DO NO HARM...

BEFORE THE BATTLE
(2007–2010)

The Good Years

Before the legal circus – before the paperwork and the sleepless nights – life was ordinary, and good.

I bought my home in 1999 for **IR£99,000** (about **€126,000**). A new two-bedroomed ground floor apartment in Clane, solid brick, nothing extravagant, very little storage, but the comforting sense that I'd earned it. I wasn't chasing the Celtic Tiger dream; my indulgences stopped at a hand-me-down stereo, a TV donated by my parents as a housewarming gift, and the occasional takeaway. I slept on a beanbag on the still bare concrete living room floor for the first few months. When I did finally get a carpet, it was the cheapest I could afford, no underlay and barely 5mm thick. No bounce or heat-retention in it at all, but at least it wasn't bare concrete anymore. All my money went into making the place habitable as soon as possible. Anything I added was strictly the cheapest option available. I furnished it over a five-year period. No brand names or gadgets, just what was practical and maybe affordable.

By November 2006 I'd stepped off the advertising industry payroll to go freelance. The risk paid off – at least initially. That first year I turned over about sixty-five grand – good money for someone in his first year. I even built a cushion of savings: six months of living costs in case work dipped. It felt like I was definitely on the way up.

In 2003, while still working full-time, I switched my mortgage to **ICS Building Society**, who sweetened the deal with a "top-up" – fifteen grand to make life easier. It sounded harmless, so I took it. That helped me with getting a few more bits and pieces for the apartment. A few years later, in 2007 at the height of the boom, they dangled another **€30,000**, and, like half the country, I bit. No one explained that each *top-up* was actually a separate mortgage with its own compounding interest. So, being completely ignorant of how the financial world works, I was now paying back a €15K mortgage over 30 years and another €30K mortgage over the same period, **added to the main one**. The bank would clean up on those loans with all the interest it would add on. One property, three accounts – triple the trouble – but at the time it looked like progress and I was oblivious to the machinations of the financial industry. That same year I treated myself to a five-year-plan Honda Civic. That was my wildest act of extravagance.

The Crash

April 2008. Driving into Dublin for a client meeting, I heard on **RTÉ** that Ireland was *"officially in recession."* By the time I parked, half the office was in a crisis meeting. Two weeks later my contract ended – there was no further work from that client.

Work enquiries quickly dried up. Clients wanted "recession rates." I had to agree to this, but even then the bookings dropped off a cliff. By Christmas I was running my own austerity programme: no gym, pension suspended, no coffees, no extras. Direct debits to charities I'd supported were cancelled, the band I played in was soon to be dissolved, even the television went. I still paid every bill and – most importantly – every mortgage instalment. When I asked ICS for a short payment moratorium – the first of four allowed under their own terms – they granted it immediately and without fuss.

So far, so civilised.

Holding the Line

By mid-2009 the slowdown had become a standstill and I had no choice but to try and get back into regular employment. After dozens of job applications I finally landed a position in Citywest, to start on the first working day of 2010. The caveat – sixty per cent less pay than my previous full-time salary from 2006. They told me during the interview that I was **lucky** even to be getting that. I felt insulted, but couldn't argue. The job was dull, the atmosphere joyless, but it was a wage. For six months I clung on.

February 2010 was the crunch point. The bank cancelled my modest **€500** overdraft without warning; my car payment bounced, and the bank took the Civic back. My brother sold me his old van for a token amount – it was ugly, but it moved. With a salary to build upon, albeit a massively reduced one, I did the maths and worked out that if I could get the second payment moratorium – again as outlined in ICS's own terms and conditions – I'd avoid slipping into arrears and get my head above the waterline. So I asked ICS for that payment break – the second of my four. This time I was stonewalled.

Weeks of silence became two months of "ongoing assessment" as the bank dragged its feet. And just as I expected, during this time my mortgage finally went into arrears. As soon as this happened, I got a phone call from ICS; a polite call centre voice named **Andrea** told me I was *now* in arrears.

"Really?" I said. "I've been waiting two months for you to approve a mortgage break I'm contractually entitled to that would have stopped that from happening."

Her "solution" was to propose that ICS take ***extra*** money from an account constantly running on fumes. I asked how that would help if the money wasn't there to begin with. She admitted it wouldn't, but said it was "protocol" and she'd been advised to offer it anyway. I told her it sounded like a box-ticking exercise rather than a genuine solution and perhaps she should put her script down and talk some actual sense. We both agreed her 'solution' wasn't remotely viable, and she promised ICS would not take the extra money from my account.

The following month, ICS took the extra money from my account despite saying they wouldn't – leaving my balance in negative figures and the bank sending me a nasty letter demanding I fix the problem. So much for Andrea's promise.

Breaking Point

I sold the last guitar I owned and the kitchen table and chairs (that's not a metaphor – the furniture was actually sold) to clear those arrears and got my account back in order for a couple of months. When an ICS manager named **Michael** finally spoke to me, he said the moratorium had been refused – because *"I didn't meet the criteria."* When I asked what those criteria were, he waffled about that information being *confidential* and then hung up.

That conversation changed everything. It was the moment I realised I was being herded into an impossible scenario. If you wait long enough, large institutions will turn your patience into the weapon they use against you. But I wasn't going to let Michael off the hook that easily. I phoned ICS every day for the next week, demanding to speak to this Michael so I could pin him down on these particular *criteria*. He avoided my calls and was always *not available*. Eventually I did get hold of him and demanded he explain these criteria. His response was that I had already had a payment holiday the year before and was not entitled to another one so soon. I asked him to point out where in the terms and conditions this was stipulated. He tried to brush that aside because I knew – and he knew – there was no such clause. After that, ICS refused to take any further calls from me and never answered any correspondence.

I'd done everything right, played by every rule, attempted proper engagement with ICS – and still ended up in the shit. It seemed the bank had deliberately pushed me into arrears. Whether that's true or not depends on your perspective, and you can draw your own conclusions; but those moratorium delays and that *solution-that-wasn't* felt like a pre-meditated plan: '*Hey, look at this guy... he's possibly heading for trouble, so let's give him a nudge to make sure he gets there*'.

By June I'd had enough of the job. My six-month probationary period was up and some of my previous clients were making contact again, so I quit the toxic office, cleaned out the apartment, packed everything into boxes, and moved to my mother's house while I tried to rent the place out at **€650 a month**. I really didn't want to rent it to strangers – it was my home – but I didn't feel as if I had a choice anymore. €650 a month from rent would get me back on level terms quickly enough.

Alas, as hard as this may be to believe now, there were no takers – none at all. The apartment sat empty for six months while ICS added "*arrears charges*" for the craic.

The Winter of Broken Pipes

Christmas 2010 brought the so-called **White Christmas** – magical for many, but rather less so for the homeowners whose pipes burst when the thaw set in.

On **St Stephen's Day**, while having family dinner at my sister's house, my next door neighbour phoned in panic: water was pouring through into his apartment from under my walls. One of the water pipes had obviously burst during the thaw.

I rushed back to the apartment and waded in ankle-deep through water-destroyed possessions – floating or submerged – until my family arrived with buckets and brushes to help. By pure luck I'd kept my insurance; so repairs were covered and furniture replaced, but my nerves were shredded.

The flood made it impossible to rent the place out now, even if I'd still wanted to. I had to run a dehumidifier for weeks to dry the apartment and replace everything the water had ruined. I saw no point now in staying at my mother's, so I moved back – water damage notwithstanding.

That winter ended whatever fantasy I'd still held about fairness and responsibility. From here, the story shifted from economics to endurance – the slow education of discovering how power really works in Ireland.

The media later dubbed people like me *"non-engaging borrowers."* I knew better. We had been trying to engage all along; it was the system that stopped answering the phone.

That's where this journey truly begins. Because what the banks started, the courts finished – or tried to.

THE SLOW CRASH OF ORDINARY LIFE (2011–2014)

From Survival to Solidarity

By 2011, survival had become a full-time job. Work came in fits and starts, income was half what it used to be, and my credit rating didn't bear thinking about. Although I was deep in arrears, I kept sending small payments to **ICS Building Society**, month after month. They accepted them without complaint or conversation – a paper handshake between two parties who no longer trusted each other. But I knew they were always adding on Mickey Mouse figures in the background. There was nothing I could do about that. I paid what I could and kept doing so.

That same year, scattered across the internet, people in similar trouble started finding each other. Social media groups were sprouting up everywhere – homeowners, small business casualties, people who'd done everything "right" and still ended up cornered. We compared letters, strategies, and hard truths. Out of those threads grew a sense that the struggle wasn't just personal; it was national.

One of those groups, **Irish Homeowners Unite**, invited me to Dublin with them to appear on *RTÉ Frontline* for a live discussion about the crash. Their chairwoman, **Caroline Lennon** – composed, quick-thinking – asked me to tell my story alongside hers.

Live television is mercilessly brief. I waited the entire recording until, at what seemed like the very last minute, Pat Kenny turned to me and said, "So, Dave, tell us your story." I condensed a year of anxiety into forty seconds: the moratorium requests, the broken system, the polite stonewalling. The moment I explained that the banks simply ignored their own *Code of Conduct on Mortgage Arrears*, Kenny turned to a Labour politician on the panel and asked:

"How do we put manners on the banks?"

The representative blustered, "Er…was this a business loan?"

The first thought that went through my mind was *What sort of moron is this?* He'd just sat through an hour of discussion about ordinary people and families in trouble with the banks.

"No," I said, "it's a mortgage… obviously!"

Cue word salad and general horseshit – nothing of substance, just a chance to get his face on the screen. By the time he'd finished speaking I couldn't remember a single thing he'd said, such was the hollow waffle he'd coughed up.

And that was the end of programme. As the studio emptied, most of the audience were lining up for selfies with Pat. I couldn't be arsed and went home feeling I'd just wasted an evening for nothing. The show had gotten its sound-bite; I was no longer needed. On the way to my car I passed that same Labour politician having a fag outside. He saw me, gave a contemptuous look, then turned his back and resumed talking to his handler. I can't even remember his name – nor can anyone else, I suspect. Just another generic, nondescript nest-featherer.

Codes, Clubs, and Cracks in the Façade

That so-called *Code of Conduct on Mortgage Arrears*, launched by the Central Bank in 2010, was lauded as a means to protect borrowers. In reality it was just lip service – an attempt to convince those in trouble that they were not being thrown to the wolves. By the time the Irish government boasted of its "success," thousands of homes had already been processed through the courts. The Code functioned perfectly for its real purpose: optics.

Through 2011 and 2012 I became involved with several grassroots groups – **Defend Our Homes League**, **People's Association Watchdog**, and later the **Anti-Eviction Taskforce (AET)**. I designed the AET logo, wrote the mission statement, and built the initial online network for each county in the Republic.

It looked like it would gain traction. But before long, people inside the organisation assumed I was going to be running the entire network. Soon various members started having petty arguments, and I very quickly started to lose heart. The idea was right; the internal politics were tiresome. I had no appetite for acting as referee in other people's arguments, but that's what I seemed to be doing more of.

One public meeting we set up was hijacked by some fringe gobshites from Louth who attempted to brand themselves as the "real" organisation for their own gain. We had actually organised the whole thing and they barged in while we were getting ready and tried to reset the agenda there and then. None of us had seen this bunch before, yet here they were trying to dictate everything. It ended with a lot of very pissed-off people, some of whom had made long trips to be there. After that, I walked away. I had enough problems of my own to deal with and didn't need this crap.

Also around that time, a farmer in Tipperary, **Seamus Sherlock**, faced eviction from his farm. Supporters built barricades of silage bales and stood guard side by side through cold nights. I slept two weekends in my van outside his gate. I was proud to stand with Seamus – just another soul caught in the machinery, trying to protect his family. He earned my enormous respect. He stood up when the odds were stacked against him and his story drew people from across the country to stand beside him. When Seamus eventually reached a deal and kept the farm, it proved the obvious: strength in numbers still mattered and standing up for yourself is important.

Good luck Seamus!

More Media and an FOI Request

In 2012 *RTÉ Prime Time* called again. I agreed, warily, to a short interview filmed during my lunch break while I was working on-site for a client in Sandymount. They wired me up in the canteen in front of my client's employees, asked a dozen questions about my situation, and in the end used thirty seconds – one, maybe two answers – heavily edited and spliced between a presenter's commentary and a nice drive-by camera shot of my apartment exterior. It was merely perfunctory – another box ticked for the public service broadcaster.

By then, the letters from **ICS Building Society** had become a weekly occurance. Each envelope carried an inflated total and a sermon about "serious arrears." Trying to establish a proper paper trail, I filed *Freedom of Information* requests on ICS. When they eventually arrived, crucial pages were missing, other pages referring to them stamped *"Not relevant."* Most were so heavily redacted that barely a single word peered through.

Apparently I didn't get to decide what was relevant.

The Coming of the Illegible Squiggle

Next came **Moriarty & Co. Solicitors**, headed by one **Brendan Moriarty** and claiming to act for ICS. They sent me a series of demanding letters, none of them properly signed—just an assortment of extravagant pen swirls. One was timed to arrive a couple of days before Christmas.

So I replied with a Christmas card:

"Dear Mr. Illegible Squiggle,

Season's greetings. Have you ever heard of goodwill to all?

Look it up.
Happy Christmas!"

When they persisted, I did the same. It became almost sport – meeting intimidation with humour until the threats stopped being frightening. Some of my replies should have been framed; I took a sarcastic stance with the Squiggles and let them know exactly what I thought of them.

Behind the sarcasm, though, an important truth emerged: even while making demands, ICS kept cashing every single postal order payment. Each one was sent by registered post, logged, tracked, and signed for at ICS headquarters. Those receipts, later entered into evidence, became the backbone of my defence.

In early 2012 I formalised the arrangement. I wrote an *Official Offer* specifying the amount, schedule, and legal intention. As far as I was concerned, their acceptance of the first payment – and every one thereafter – made the arrangement contractually binding in practice. Whatever legal jargon they used later, the facts were simple: **I paid every month; they happily took the money.**

For two years I kept it up, doubling payments when I could. Finally, Squiggles & Co sent one final letter demanding I pay €150,000 within seven days or hand the keys over. I ignored them and then it all went silent; I didn't hear from **Bren & Co.** for months. The peace held until July 2014, when a new logo appeared on a familiar envelope: **Whitney Moore Solicitors.**

Same stilted tone, fancier letterhead – and then the names and professional pictures on the Whitney Moore Solicitors website: **Brendan Moriarty** and **Karen Molloy**, freshly transplanted from their old firm. The Squiggles had gone up in the world. The letter warned that I would "be served soon." I sent it back with a short note of farewell, though the actual wording was a bit more, shall we say… *street level.*

Then they went quiet for ten months.

During this lull, in August 2014, a Civil Bill for Possession had apparently been filed. It was another nine months before I discovered it. Apparently they just *'forgot'* to tell me. Or maybe the dog ate their letters. Whatever the reason, I heard nary a peep out of the new Squiggles while shenanigans were obviously going on in the background. By January 2015 they had appeared **ex parte** before the Circuit Court in Naas and quietly replaced **ICS Building Society** with **The Governor and Company of the Bank of Ireland**. No notice to me. No chance to object. I only discovered this months later, after the fact.

It wasn't until April 2015 that I discovered my home was the subject of proceedings that had advanced without my knowledge.

It wouldn't be the last time this happened.

SERVICE WITH A SNEER (2015)

Cometh the Hour, Cometh the Cardigan (20 April 2015)

Monday night, just after nine. Dinner half-eaten, and I'm late getting back from an on-site booking, hence eating late. Someone rapped hard on the window – the code friends, family and neighbours used because the front buzzer was broken. I opened the communal door expecting someone I knew.

Instead stood a man in his fifties, a cardigan and grim expression in place.

"I'm looking for Mr. David Morrissey."

"Who are you?"

"I'm with Whitney Moore Solicitors."

Without another word he hurled what could only be described as half a rainforest of paper through the open doorway, barked "You're served," and disappeared toward his car at jogging speed. The nice man hadn't even cared that the inside hallway was a communal area, not my property at all – and none of the papers had touched me or anything I owned. But he skipped off like a happy twat all the same, probably looking forward to collecting his fee and getting pissed.

I was annoyed at myself; a) for not checking I knew whoever it was who was trying to get me to open the door; b) for actually opening the door; and c) for allowing this git to throw his crap past me.

I took a quick photo of the papers lying where they'd landed – proof of how "service" looked in practice – then, realising I couldn't leave them there without annoying the neighbours, gathered them up and started reading into the night. Mr. McCardigan would obviously have known I couldn't leave a huge pile of papers lying there, so he was covered.

The scattered bundle contained a **Civil Bill for Possession**, dated 13 August 2014 – nine months old. Inside was a note that an **ex parte hearing** had taken place on 26 January 2015. No notice, no summons, no idea it even existed. Then I noticed that the court date had already been set, **Monday 27 April 2015 – four working days away.**

I had no time whatsoever to prepare. They'd held onto the papers for nine months and then fecked them at me at the very, VERY last minute. Lovely. We weren't even in the courtroom yet and already the sleeveen tactics had started.

The Registrar's Court (27 April 2015)

The few days before the hearing were a blur of Google searches and sleepless nights. I had no solicitor, no script, and no real clue what I was walking into. The plan was simple: explain lack of notice, request time to file an affidavit, and try and get my bearings. What I did discover was that the first time in court on a possession case is an automatic adjournment. Nothing is discussed in terms of the affidavits and the case does not move forward. The first listing is essentially just making sure the parties are present and ready to proceed.

Well I ***wasn't*** ready to proceed. How can you be ready to defend yourself with just a week's notice, when you also have work commitments to complete and no chance to set time aside to get the head around all the paperwork – to say nothing about even being able to file a reply? I wasn't having it!

I'd never been in a court before. Naas Circuit Court that Monday morning looked like another world – dozens of possession cases, only a handful of defendants and more black-caped individuals than you'd see at a Batman convention.

A voice asked, "Is there a David Morrissey in the room?"

I located the voice and walked over to a guy in a creased blue suit. "I'm David Morrissey. Who are you?"

"I'm acting for the Plaintiff," he replied.

Funny name, that, I thought.

Mr. Actingfortheplaintiff asked if we could have a quiet word outside the room. I nodded and we moved outside to the corridor. He never actually told me his name but assured me with mock civility that they'd be "asking the court for an adjournment so you'll have time to prepare."

"How thoughtful," I said, "the first appearance *always* gets an automatic adjournment. Were you hoping I didn't know that?"

The mock civility abruptly vanished; he walked off without another word. Introducing Mr. Luke Hanahoe, ladies and gentlemen!

When the case was called, the Registrar confirmed exactly that: an automatic adjournment. I raised the farce of service – the flying paper routine, the last minute delivery – but she replied, "Well, you're here, so you must have been served." I replied that if you count throwing reams of paper into a communal area as service without even verifying someone's identity, does that actually count as proper service? She just repeated that "You're here." Damned if you do, damned if you don't.

I then told her that something had happened in this room without my knowledge back in January and I wanted to know exactly what it was. She directed Mr. Actingfortheplaintiff to instruct Whitney Moore to **re-serve me properly by registered post** and **provide details of the ex parte hearing.** A small victory.

Adjourned to **June 2015.**

The Registrar's Court (22 June 2015)[1]

Mere days before the new listing a heavy envelope hit the letterbox – despite a full two months having elapsed – postmarked **Friday 12 June** but not actually sent out until **Tuesday 16 June**, because it arrived on **Wednesday 17 June.** It was a classic scumbag tactic: frank it early, hang onto it for another couple of days, then send it at the last possible moment. Whatever the intention, the result was the same – I had almost no time to prepare. Even at this early stage I was sensing a pattern emerging.

Inside the thick package were "updated" affidavits, now naming the plaintiff not as ICS but as **The Governor and Company of the Bank of Ireland.** I'd never borrowed a cent from them, yet they now claimed ownership of my home.

The courtroom was packed again – this Batman convention attracting even more attendees than the last one. Mr. Actingfortheplaintiff was present again, stood to announce that all proofs were "in order" and requested immediate possession. I objected – late service and no time to respond. Same tired answer from the Registrar: "You're here, so you must have been served."

The thought of properly pushing back over the last-minute service hadn't yet occurred to me. I was still far too inexperienced. I should have stood my ground and not engaged their arguments. I would have done if I'd been a bit more court savvy. That would come later. Pushing back on late service would have shut them down and kicked things back further.

---

[1] The exchanges in this section are fully verifiable from the DAR transcript: 150622 The Governor and Company of the Bank of Ireland v. David Morrissey

The Registrar asked if I'd been making payments. "Yes," I said, "every month for over three years." Hanahoe tried to cut in; I raised my voice just enough to get the truth recorded before he could continue. After stuttering about with buzzwords like "unsustainable" and "long-standing arrears", he finally conceded that the bank had been receiving the payments. The Registrar nodded: "Record that." I pointed out that this fact did not appear anywhere on the Plaintiff's paperwork.

Note that before you go any further. It was acknowledged – on the record – that I had been making regular payments for over three years. Acknowledged by both the Registrar <u>and</u> the bank's legal representative in court, Luke Hanahoe – on the record. Noted? Good!

When substitution came up, I explained I'd never been told ICS had sold the loan, had no account with Bank of Ireland, and a continuing contract with ICS. Hanahoe insisted, "ICS no longer exists."

I asked for the original mortgage documents proving any lawful transfer. Slightly taken aback that a layman even knew to ask, the Registrar directed Whitney Moore to **furnish all relevant documents within two weeks** and to have a "relationship manager" (a mythical bank staff member as it turned out) contact me. Adjourned to **October 2015.**

I left court shaky but proud: the payments were acknowledged, the documentation ordered, and my own voice finally on the record.

Some actual progress? I thought so.

The Registrar's Court (12 October 2015)

By autumn I could see the tactic clearly – delay, exhaust, repeat. Each affidavit arrived days before the sitting, freshly dated but days, weeks or even months old. The aim was to keep me scrambling. Every hearing cost time, wages, and sanity.

Despite instructions given to them in June, Whitney Moore *never* furnished the documents the court had ordered. Nor did any mythical "relationship manager" appear. All instructions casually ignored – and it wouldn't be the last time. Meanwhile, the affidavits still listed **ICS Building Society** as payee even as the bank's team swore it had "ceased to exist."

Between those two listings, I drove to Dublin and checked the address on an affidavit of service by one **Francis Craven** – apparently the real identity of the walking cardigan. He had never identified himself to me, nor I to him, yet on his affidavit he claimed we both did just that. Mr. McCardigan swore – under penalty of perjury – that his address was "Suite 15, Isolde's Tower, Dublin 8."

The problem is, there *was* no Suite 15 anywhere in Isolde's Tower. A resident I spoke to there confirmed it didn't exist. I showed him the Cardigan's affidavit with the address listed at the top and he said that "whoever yer man is, is actin' the bollix!" The same resident kindly allowed me to inspect the post boxes in the complex and nowhere was there a "Suite 15" to be found. It may well have been the whiff coming off the nearby Liffey, but I could definitely smell fish. Time to get the walking cardigan into court to explain himself.

I sent Frankie Baby a summons to appear before Naas Court, posted to Suite 15, Isolde's Tower, Dublin 8 – that was the address he had put on his own affidavit, after all – under penalty of perjury. That summons bounced back from An Post[2] to the court office in Naas labelled *"no such address."* Naas court office then forwarded it back to me stamped *"no such address."*

So the address Frankie of the Clan Cardigan had sworn to on his affidavit of service was demonstrably false. I made a note to tell the court exactly that.

Perjury? Hmmm… if true then that's a bit naughty.

In Naas, the Registrar took the list and proceeded as before. Hanahoe opened smoothly, once again declaring every affidavit impeccable. I pointed out the non-existent address, the back-dated letters, and the failure to produce originals despite clear previous instructions given back in June. The Registrar, clearly not in the least bit arsed, noted my "concerns on record" and moved the case to the **Judge's List.**

Translation: the Registrar *really* didn't want to deal with this and was only interested in getting it off her list.

I was beginning to see quite clearly that this wasn't about facts, evidence or proof at all – it was a rubber stamping exercise.

[2] Verifiable by An Post return envelope retained as proof. If in doubt of its authenticity, I am more than happy to produce it.

End of Year

On paper it looked routine – three brief hearings, a few directions, several adjournments. In reality each one cost days of preparation and the better part of my nerves. I still posted payments every month, logged every receipt, and methodically built the archive. By contrast however, the other side ignored each and every instruction handed out by the court and nothing was ever done about it, even after it had been raised – on the record – by myself. I was definitely seeing the pattern.

Somewhere along the line I understood the real design of the process: **the process is the punishment.** You don't have to lose a case to be broken by it; you just have to keep turning up and have another part of your faith shattered.

The next step was beyond the Registrar now. The first appearance before a Judge was fixed for **January 2016.**

After four years of quiet attrition, the real fight was about to begin.

JUDGE DREAD
(2016–2017)

Before Judge O'Sullivan (26 January 2016)

My first day in front of a Judge.

I half-expected stern silence and Greek/Latin legalese. Instead I got Judge Terence O'Sullivan – decent, even disarmingly human, capable of a smile when things weren't too heavy. The difference between Registrars and Judges – at least *this* Judge – became obvious within five minutes: the Registrar looked for quick outcomes; Judge O'Sullivan listened.

Whitney Moore fielded a new barrister alongside Mr. Actingfortheplaintiff, one of those fresh-minted types climbing the ladder by collecting easy homeowner scalps. Luke Hanahoe hovered in front of her like a prompter feeding lines. Before anything even started he leaned across and handed me a thick, wire-bound indexed folder. I accepted it, wondering what new fairy tales it contained.

Right out of the gate, counsel tried theatre.
She announced that I'd "summoned two witnesses,"
then declared solemnly that "Whitney Moore is not
a man or woman but the name of a firm."

I interjected: "If that's correct, Judge, how can the name *Whitney Moore* have a human, blue-ink signature at the bottom of legal documents? Is someone forging Whitney's signature?" That gem drew polite chuckles from down the back of the room. The Bruce Wayne brigades in the room, not having a sense of humour, wound in their chins.

I need to explain this further: I had tried to summon Frankie McCardigan to court, but that failed because he gave a bogus address – on a sworn affidavit (under penalty of perjury). At the same time I also summonsed Whitney Moore to appear before the court, because someone called *Whitney Moore* was signing letters by hand. It stood to reason that *Whitney Moore* existed as a living, breathing man or woman, and I had questions to put to him/her.

I honestly wasn't expecting this to go anywhere or advance my case, but I wanted to lay down a marker – that I was examining everything in their paperwork. The Judge raised an eyebrow and said nothing; my fellow defendants chuckled quietly; I marked an unofficial first point on my scorecard.

Then came the real business. The matter of service was in dispute. The affidavit of service had a bogus address on it and I could prove quite easily that it was false. An Post itself had confirmed it – unless of course evidence by An Post itself somehow wasn't credible. Immediately, the Judge refused to grant any possession order and said flatly that the plaintiff's case would **not proceed** until the matter of service was explained and proven. He instructed Whitney Moore to clarify it before the next date.

Clear as day: adjournment by default, serious questions still hanging over a dodgy affidavit of service.

While I had the floor, I drove the knife in gently:

"Judge, the plaintiff has refused repeatedly to acknowledge my written requests for the original mortgage documents. The plaintiff has also failed, refused, or neglected to comply with clear instructions given by the Registrar when it came before the court last year. Those instructions were clear and explicit."

He asked, "Which documents precisely, Mr. Morrissey?"

I listed them, reading slowly so they'd go into the record. Then he asked why I insisted on originals.

"Because, Judge, the plaintiff still hasn't proved ownership of any mortgage when it started these proceedings. They've produced copies – copies that could have been run off last week or ten years ago. *Only originals prove title.* And they're silent because they can't find them."

To my surprise he let me develop the point unhindered, and then, unprompted, the bank's own barrister blurted, "Judge, those documents do exist and can be produced if required."

Judge O'Sullivan cut her off.

"It would hardly be fair on Mr. Morrissey to view such material 'on the hoof.' Mr. Morrissey, would you prefer to inspect them by appointment?"

"Absolutely, Judge – and I'd like to bring a witness to confirm they're genuine."

Granted. Formal instruction: appointment to be made to view the original documents at the solicitor's premises before the next hearing. Again… **a formal instruction from the Judge.**

I left court lighter by a stone, amazed to find manners and fairness in a courtroom. Judge O'Sullivan gave me space to speak and kept counsel tight on the leash. If the legal merchants hated me before, they despised me now – another hearing postponed, costs mounting, their payday delayed by one argumentative lay litigant learning as he went along.

Before Judge Griffin (10 May 2016)[3]

By the time May rolled around, my patience with Whitney Moore was gone. It had been four and a half months since Judge O'Sullivan's directions and nothing had been done – no inspection arranged, no explanation of the dodgy service, nothing. It was also nearly a full year since the Registrar had instructed the plaintiff to assign a relationship manager to contact me, and that hadn't happened either. It was obvious the plaintiff's solicitors were going to stall until forced into a corner.

So I was going to force them into that corner. I had filed a **motion for discovery** some weeks earlier; it was clear to me that Whitney Moore had no intention

[3] The exchanges in this section are fully verifiable from the DAR transcript: 160510 The Governor & Company of the Bank of Ireland v. David Morrissey

of allowing me to view the originals, despite Judge O'Sullivan's order, so I would seek to have the court compel them instead. They'd left me no choice.

When I arrived at Naas Courthouse that Tuesday morning, the place was heaving. It was the last week of term and half the county seemed to be queued outside Court 2. This was the older courtroom downstairs, and it felt it – dark, church-like, all it was missing was an organ in the balcony.

I took a bench near the front and spotted Luke Hanahoe across the aisle. Beside him stood another barrister I hadn't seen before – early thirties, cape draped, clearly ready to rock. He flicked through a lever arch file fat enough to contain three copies of the Lord of the Rings, obviously rehearsing his first line.

When the case was finally called just before lunch, it began the same way they all did – counsel launching straight into a well-scripted monologue before I'd even reached the bench. It was as though the Judge was there to authenticate a formality, not hear a dispute. Because I had a motion before the court I was entitled to speak first, but they'd pre-empted that by trying to move their case immediately, even though Judge O'Sullivan had forbidden it. But this was a new Judge, fresh to the case, and O'Sullivan wasn't around, so…

"Judge, this is a straight-forward possession matter; all proofs are in order, and the accounts are –"

Judge Griffin interrupted him, a flicker of a raised eyebrow above his reading glasses.

"Let's deal with basic matters first," he said dryly. "When was the last payment made by the defendant?"

Without hesitation, as though reading from a playbook, the barrister replied:

"Judge, the last payment on the first account was on the 30th of November 2012."

That was a defining moment in the case. I stood there for about ten seconds, open-mouthed, unable to believe what I'd just heard said on the record.

Four years ago?

"Judge, that statement is wholly inaccurate. I've been making payments every single month – the last one less than two weeks ago."

Griffin looked at me for a long moment, caught off-guard by the interruption, but instead of admonishing me he said kindly:

"We'll come back to you, Mr. Morrissey. Sit down for a moment."

The counsel, perhaps thinking he could drown me in detail, continued reading from his sheet:

"On the second account, payment was last made 19 January 2011; on the third, 5 February 2011."

***Five** years ago?*

That did it. I reached into the black expanding file on the bench beside me and pulled out a folder I'd prepared precisely for this moment – **Proof of Payments.** Inside sat years of relentless record-keeping: carbon copies of postal orders, registered post receipts, track-and-trace printouts, and An Post signature sheets with delivery dates and initials [4].

"Judge, may I hand these to the court Registrar, please?"

Griffin nodded. The papers travelled down the bench and into his hands. He began reading in silence. After a few moments he looked up, then back down again, as the extent of the record became clear—every payment stapled to its receipt, every registered post receipt proving delivery.

"Mr. Morrissey, when was your most recent payment?"

"The twenty fifth of April, Judge, by registered post. You should find the record of that payment at the front end of the documents."

He opened my folder and found the corresponding entry. "Yes, I see it here." He flipped back a few pages, compared receipts, cross-checked dates and signatures. Then he turned to the barrister:

"On your side's evidence, when was the last payment?"

"Based on the statements of account we've reviewed, Judge, 30 November 2012."

And these statements were exhibited in affidavit form?"

"They were, Judge."

Griffin tapped the bench with his pen: once, twice.

---

[4] Each and every one of the payments receipts, copies of each dated postal order and registered post receipt have been stored and can be produced to prove their authenticity… in their entirety. Be in no doubt – I kept absolutely everything.

"If I were to rely solely on your affidavit, it would appear that this man hasn't paid a cent in nearly four years. Yet these documents clearly show regular monthly payments right up to last month."

The silence was deafening for about ten seconds. Then the barrister stammered.

"Judge, if I might explain – the statements show very low amounts compared to the original mortgage payments, and there may have been a gap –"

"Whether they're low isn't the point," Griffin interrupted. "They're payments, and they're consistent. Are they acknowledged anywhere in the plaintiff's affidavits?"

"No, Judge, not directly."

"Not directly," Griffin repeated flatly. "So the affidavits omit years of actual payments?"

Batman-lite looked to Hanahoe for rescue. Mr. Actingfortheplaintiff stared at the table in silence. He'd been in every hearing. He *knew.*

"Counsel, you will prepare a **supplemental affidavit** listing each payment received and accepted. I want the specific dates, the amounts, and how they were allocated. I am *not* satisfied with what's before me."

He turned back to me.

"Mr. Morrissey, you've kept very thorough records."

"I learned the hard way, Judge," I said, probably sounding more tired than triumphant.

"Have you any objection to those being copied for the plaintiff's side?"

"None at all, Judge – though they should already *have* them if they're honest about what came in."

The faintest twitch of a smile crossed his face before he turned back to counsel.

"Your client will acknowledge every one of these entries. If this man had not appeared in court today, I would have had no reason to believe any payments existed. You're looking for a possession order against this man and you've come into this court leaving out information that is crucial and could potentially sway a decision. That cannot happen again."

He set down the file decisively.

"The matter will be adjourned to allow the supplemental affidavit to be sworn."

Hanahoe kept his head down while his junior rifled through papers that suddenly looked flimsy. He murmured something about arrears calculations. Griffin halted him with a hand.

"We'll deal with arrears once the facts are correct. Getting the facts right is not optional."

Before the Judge could finish, I asked about the motion already before the court, as it was clearly not going to be heard that day. Judge Griffin assured me it would be dealt with at the next adjourned hearing. I thanked him, and that was that.

The Judge had said it aloud– on the record. What was contained in the bank's affidavits did not match the truth. They had tried to conceal years of documented payments from the court and had been caught red-handed.

Outside, I sat on the courthouse steps for ten minutes trying to process it all. The truth had finally surfaced, but I was angry that it had taken a year of hearings and a suitcase full of receipts to prove something the bank and its legal team already knew.

That morning in May 2016 changed everything. From then on, the plaintiff could never again depend on unchallenged affidavits (or so I thought). Every number sworn would have to line up with the documents I'd just put into evidence – and that terrified them.

For that one morning under Judge Griffin, the truth was plain on the record: my payments were real, continuous, and deliberately omitted from the bank's sworn statements. No amount of future spin could erase that moment. Luke Hanahoe vanished entirely following this listing. From here on it was a barrister advocating for the plaintiff in the circuit court until it concluded. Hanahoe and myself wouldn't cross paths again in court, but he'd hear from me a few years later.

Before Judge Fergus (26 July 2016)

The Griffin hearing left me stunned – and, once I'd had time to digest it, angry. When a Judge says on record that affidavits omit critical facts, solicitors can't ignore it. Suddenly every letter from **Whitney Moore** sounded frantic: requests for clarification, cautious phrasing, the careful "without prejudice" tone of people trying to redraw a line they'd already crossed.

Judge Griffin had clearly caught them being dishonest right in front of him, yet there'd been no sanction other than a mild rebuke. They were told to clean up their figures, not explain how they'd come to be false in the first place. If I'd had a feel for courtroom tactics, I'd have moved to strike out the case there and then and asked for a disciplinary inquiry. They'd lied to a Judge's face and been found out – still no censure, no consequences – and my **motion for discovery of the original documentation**, in tandem with clear instructions given months earlier by Judge O'Sullivan, never even surfaced.

The instruction to file a supplemental affidavit should have been straightforward: admit the payments, list the dates, correct the falsehood, and move on. But when the "supplement" arrived, it was the same old shite– a clean-looking PDF repeating the same figures, with a single cosmetic paragraph tacked on about "difficulties reconciling certain remittances." In other words, nothing had been conceded.

Meanwhile, the paperwork morphed again. At the top of one new affidavit the name *ICS Building Society* simply vanished, replaced by *The Governor and Company of the Bank of Ireland* with no explanation of when the substitution was actually granted. When I matched the document's footer date against the Land Registry entries, the timing made no sense: the bank claiming to own the loan didn't even hold the charge at the time. And Bank of Ireland's name, or *any* of its legal names, never appeared on that folio and to this day, never has.

Adding to the motion for discovery, I filed another – to move the proceedings from summary to **plenary hearing** – as I now had more than enough to raise: fraudulent service, ignored instructions, and misrepresentation to the court verging on perjury.

The next hearing was listed for **26 July 2016**, the last working week before the courts shut for the summer break. Naas Courthouse looked fit to burst: even the corridors were packed, Batman cos players everywhere and their intended victims forming a line down the stairs.

I was there early, propped against the same wall where I'd waited back in 2015, still carrying the black expanding case that now needed a seat of its own. A couple of people recognised me – a rare sight, a defendant who kept showing up. One older man whispered, *"Fair play; you showed them up the last time."*

Unfortunately, to my dismay, Judge Griffin wasn't hearing the case that day – making it now three different Judges in as many sittings. I was getting more than a bit fed up with this constant shuffling of Judges. It meant that each time a new Judge heard the case, I had to frantically try and recap what had gone on previously before the other side got going. I have no doubt that this rotating of Judges was a welcome development for my opponents and they'd use it to full effect. After all, a new Judge coming in to an already running case cannot possibly remember the nuances of what had gone on before.

When my number was finally called, I could barely squeeze into Court 3. **Judge Karen Fergus** took her seat, radiating the determination of someone who planned to clear the entire list before lunch. Beside the plaintiff's bench stood yet another new barrister, back stiff, young, probably fresh off the farm. But there was no sign of Luke Hanahoe.

She started reading before I reached the front.

"Judge, this is a straightforward possession matter. The defendant – "

I didn't even wait. They'd deflected Judge Griffin by speaking first; I wasn't letting it happen again.

"Judge, I object immediately. Two motions stand before this Court – one for **Discovery** and another seeking to convert the proceedings to a **Plenary Hearing.** They must be heard first."

The words landed heavy enough to still the gallery for a second. The Judge rolled her eyes - actually.

"Motions – what motions precisely, Mr. Morrissey?"

I handed up my notices – four pages each, stapled, signed, served weeks earlier. She studied them, expression balanced between disbelief and irritation. *He knows what he's doing,* I could almost hear her think, *and that's inconvenient.*

"And on what grounds are you seeking these?"

"Judge, the plaintiff's affidavit of service by Francis Craven is very possibly fraudulent. Judge O'Sullivan already ruled that this case was not to proceed until that matter was resolved. That has not been done. In addition, repeated orders and instructions given to the plaintiff have been ignored – production of original documents, and the supplemental affidavit ordered in May remains non-compliant."

She leaned back slightly, almost amused.

"Mr. Morrissey, you do understand that alleging fraud is quite serious?"

"I do, Judge – as did Judge O'Sullivan, which is why he stopped the case until it was addressed."

Before she could reply, the plaintiff's barrister jumped in, quick and shrill:

"Judge, Judge O'Sullivan previously ruled Mr. Morrissey's motion irrelevant."

It was pure invention – my motion **hadn't even existed** when O'Sullivan sat back in January[5].

"THAT IS A COMPLETE FABRICATION," I said, voice tightening. "They're claiming the Judge made a ruling on a motion that didn't exist."

---

[5] A copy of the Notion of Motion, the Grounding Affidavit and their exact filing dates, stamped by the Court Office, can be produced if doubt exists.

"LET-HER-SPEAK!!!" Judge Fergus bellowed. The interjection hit like a slap and it bloody annoyed me. I'd just caught their barrister making a ridiculous and obviously untruthful claim, and the Judge decided to roar at *me* instead of addressing it. I was sensing serious bias coming from the bench.

The barrister reddened and began reading – almost chanting – from the fresh **Affidavit of Ruth Tracey**: paragraph after paragraph of procedural boilerplate, legal yadda, pseudo-English waffle – music to the judge's ears.

She referred repeatedly to my home as a *Principal Private Residence.* I corrected her quietly the first time: "It's my dwelling." The second time I said it louder. By the third, the Judge's head jerked up.

"We have dealt with that expression, Mr. Morrissey. Not another word."

Her demeanour was adversarial from the start, and I knew nothing I said would help. So I stood silent and counted each paragraph until the recital finally ended.

Then came the bank's reliable chorus line: arrears, sustainability, balance due, yadda, yadda. The Judge leaned slightly toward me, clearly gearing up to explore those figures, eager to restore control after my interruption. But I hadn't finished.

"Judge, are we going to deal with the motions and potential fraud that I've now mentioned twice today, or are Judge O'Sullivan's instructions being ignored again?"

There it was – lodged on the record where no later edit could delete it. The silence afterward was heavy enough to weigh on the bench. Fergus exhaled, glanced at her list – twenty-five-odd cases still to hear – and realised she couldn't bury this in a ten minute slot without risking appeal.

"Given the issues raised, this matter will have to go to a **full hearing.**"

She instructed the clerk to allocate roughly two hours when the lists reopened after the break.

The barrister started protesting immediately.

"Judge, this case has been running since 2014 – it's in everyone's interests to have it concluded today."

Judge Fergus ignored her, still pencilling dates. Her look said what her words didn't: *the banks have used up their courtesy for the term.*

The barrister tried one final move – it was desperate and pathetic.

"It's really in Mr. Morrissey's best interests to finalise matters today rather than prolong the inevitable."

I looked straight at her.

"***My** best interests* involve a possession order being given against me today? Really?"

I couldn't help remembering a line from *The Outlaw Josey Wales*. Somehow it seemed appropriate. "Don't piss down my back and tell me it's raining." I could almost smell the horseshit.

As papers gathered up around me, Judge Fergus delivered the inevitable warning every self-represented defendant eventually hears:

"Mr. Morrissey, I would strongly advise you to obtain professional representation. If this hearing goes against you, the consequences will be serious."

I answered as evenly as I could.

"With respect, Judge, I'm quite capable of defending my case – and the party in trouble here isn't me."

That ended it. She adjourned to the autumn for scheduling of the full hearing. No possession order, no summary decision. Just more waiting.

Outside I stood on the steps and calmed the jets for a few minutes. I'd halted them again; but was frustrated that there was no consistency in the listings. Three different Judges – so far, and three days in court trying to convince each Judge that the other side was clearly ***at it***. And yet I wondered if I was making any progress at all?

The Griffin moment had changed everything. They could no longer claim ignorance about what the bank had omitted. Yet within their affidavits, silence had already shown itself to be their most successful tactic. They would bank on silence again.

I also realised that the bank and its legal team were exploiting the situation of a fresh Judge hearing the case each time it came before the court. They were counting on everything being re-set to zero and pressing on with their case, before I could get a word in. By the time it came before Judge Fergus, I was quick to step in and correct the record by pointing out what had gone on before. To each new Judge, this was a fresh case. It was incumbent upon me to let them know that it wasn't and bring them up to speed. Judge Fergus clearly didn't like that and from my own observation, didn't even try to hide her irritation.

The "full hearing" promised by Judge Fergus would never happen that autumn. Indeed it wouldn't happen at all. It was delayed into the new year, re-listed, and finally handled by yet another Judge – **James O'Donoghue** – the man who, a year later, would sign the possession order.

That day in July 2016 was really the last time anyone in authority still had the chance to stop the rot properly. They could have examined the false address, the disputed affidavit, and the missing documents and payments already flagged by Judge O'Sullivan and Judge Griffin. Instead, they continued to kick it down the road.

Meanwhile, earlier that same day – in the same courtroom – before the same judge...

One thing, entirely unrelated to my own case but which, for me, highlighted the absurdity of the court system, certainly stood out that day. About half an hour before mine, a case was heard involving a minor suing Kildare County Council, through his mother, over an accident in a public playground. The child – let's call him 'Little Johnny' – was perhaps twelve or thirteen.

Counsel quickly outlined the distress and injury caused by the accident and explained that Little Johnny had been left physically scarred. From the description, it sounded serious enough. Judge Fergus asked where the scarring was.

"On his forehead."

She asked Little Johnny to approach the bench so she could see it.

He came forward. She couldn't see it.

He came closer. Still nothing.

Finally, Little Johnny was standing right in front of her. The judge looked directly at his forehead, tilted her head a few times and asked for his hair to be brushed back. With sunlight streaming into the courtroom and illuminating the alleged scene of devastation, she eventually declared:

"Ah yes, I can see a scar there now."

As Little Johnny returned to the pew directly in front of us, I began questioning my own eyesight. Having had my attention firmly directed to the spot by this forensic examination, I couldn't see any discernible scar either. Perhaps specialised judicial training was required. Or a magnifying glass. Possibly both.

Apparently satisfied that Little Johnny would have to carry this terrible burden through life, Judge Fergus asked counsel what compensation he considered appropriate.

"We're asking for €15,000, Judge."
"Granted."

Little Johnnys mother beamed.

Perhaps surprised by how smoothly negotiations had progressed, counsel decided to **really** chance his arm.

"Judge, may we also ask that, in order to aid in his recovery, the child be given extra help during his recuperation?"

"What kind of help?"
"A PlayStation and some disks."
"What kind of disks? Are these educational programmes?"
"Er, yes, Judge. Educational programmes."
"How many would he need?"
"Oh, five or ten would probably suffice."
"Granted."

And with that, Little Johnnys treatment plan was complete. €15,000, a PlayStation and somewhere between five and ten absolutely, definitely, unquestionably educational programmes – for the PlayStation.

The mother beamed a second time. The barrister looked suitably pleased with proceedings. Little Johnny, presumably contemplating the long and difficult road to recovery ahead of him, departed with his entourage, the three of them having demonstrated that Christmas does not, apparently, come only in December.

I can only hope Little Johnny recovered without requiring the extensive plastic surgery his condition clearly warranted, and that his intensive programme of PlayStation-based rehabilitation eventually enabled him to overcome his ordeal, with those 'educational programmes' (for the PlayStation) eventually helping him on to third level. Having witnessed first-hand how smoothly the gravy train could roll, he probably studied 'Law' and went into the legal profession himself.

Or am I just being too cynical?

County Registrar Call-Over (14 December 2016)[6]

So I found myself back before the county Registrar, if only at a call-over. The case was reached mid-list. **Finola Martin BL**, making her debut here for **Whitney Moore Solicitors**, appeared for the plaintiff; I was present in person.

When it was called, Ms. Martin told the Registrar she was appearing on behalf of Whitney Moore and that her instructions were to have the matter fixed for hearing – **"a day and a half."**

The Registrar confirmed the estimate. I asked to have it repeated, saying I'd previously understood it would be about two hours. The Registrar replied evenly, "Well, whatever anyway," and selected **3 February 2017** as the first available date.

Both sides confirmed availability. The case was noted for hearing and adjourned. That was all that happened: no argument, no discussion of documents, just the fixing of a date.

[6] The exchanges in this section along with times, dates and agreed duration of the scheduled 'full hearing' are fully verifiable from the DAR transcript: 161214 The Governor and Company of the Bank of Ireland v. David Morrissey

THE HEARING THAT WASN'T (2017)

Before Judge O'Donoghue (3 February 2017)[7]

The fourth different Judge in as many hearings. So much for consistency. At least, I thought, I have a day and a half now to get my arguments across. There's no rush, no need for me to interrupt or act rashly.

When my case was finally called before **Judge O'Donoghue**, it was in a surprisingly nearly empty courtroom. I'd been used to overflowing, claustrophobic settings up to now, so this was unusual. The reason for the sparse attendance was down to this day being allocated for a proper hearing, so aside from my case, nothing else was due to be heard. **Finola Martin BL** again appeared solo for the Bank of Ireland. The Registrar announced the listing:

"The Governor and Company of the Bank of Ireland versus David Morrissey."

Judge O'Donoghue began briskly, asking how long it would take.

"Half a day," said the barrister.

[7] The exchanges in this section are fully verifiable from the DAR transcript: 170203 The Governor and Company of the Bank of Ireland v. David Morrissey

He nodded, already impatient. "Right then, let's get on with it."

If you skip back two pages, you'll see that it was Finola Martin herself that was instructed to ask for a day and a half. It was that very timeframe I had been preparing for. I smelled another rat immediately.

I told the Judge straight away that the time allocated to the hearing was actually a day and a half, not a half day as Martin had just told him and he should check the files in front of him for confirmation of that fact. Silence.

I then told him I opposed the bank's application, that I was acting for myself, and that the bank's case rested on **fraudulent affidavits, instructions all being casually ignored on the plaintiff's side** and **omitted figures and facts from the plaintiff's affidavits**. He cut me off almost instantly.

"Yes, right, okay. Very good. Now, I'm not going to listen to a day of nonsense, I can tell you that."

That single dismissal set the tone. The word *fraud* had closed the shutters.

I asked whether he had read my affidavit – long though it was, I'd collected a great deal of information, carefully built on the record of the previous two years. He looked over his glasses.

"No. I don't know whether I've time to read all that today."

Then, shuffling pages without looking at me, he added, almost absently:

"I've no interest in waffle and nonsense."

In case anyone missed it, that was how a sitting Judge described an affidavit he had **not even read**: *"I've no interest in waffle and nonsense."* It would have been lovely to find myself in front of a judge prepared to listen to both sides of the argument. A pity I didn't get that.

It's remarkable how months of work can be erased by one sentence. He hadn't read a line, yet knew exactly what it contained. I could almost smell the contempt.

At that point I tried to raise the fact that there were **two motions** before the court which had already gone through several listings without ever being heard. Judge O'Donoghue slapped that down.

"We're not hearing those motions today."

It was more than obvious to me that this Judge had no intention of allowing me to present my case; he was going to ignore every single point I tried to make, and wanted to be out of there as quickly as possible. Maybe he had a date lined up?

The next thing he did was dismiss my argument over service and I got the same old "you're here so you must have accepted service" line again. The Judge utterly dismissed Craven's false address as an irrelevance, saying that my appearance legally cured that defect. I wasn't aware that my mere presence could wipe away a false statement placed on affidavit. Just shows what I know.

From then on the hearing became arithmetic – arrears, instalments, property value; nothing about legitimacy.

When Ms. Martin conceded that her arrears affidavit was months out of date, Judge O'Donoghue *suddenly* cared: a technical irregularity. Procedural neatness mattered; sworn truth did not.

"Well now, I'll have to adjourn it. We'll need an up-to-date affidavit."

That was it. The case was adjourned – not because the defence had merit, but because **their paperwork** wasn't tidy enough. At the same time, my paperwork had been refused and not allowed to be opened to the court.

Before closing, he sneered down from his pulpit:

"The writing's on the wall for you, Mr. Morrissey. You should look at it with a bit of realism."

I wondered how he knew the writing was on the wall for me. It was an impressive conclusion to reach without first hearing the defence.

When I left court that day, I finally understood that **efficiency** and **justice** are not the same thing.

The day-and-a-half hearing I'd prepared for was over in about fifteen minutes. My arguments were never heard. Strangely though, the plaintiff's were.

"I've no interest in waffle and nonsense."

"No. I don't know whether I've time to read all that today."

He had plenty of time – mine was the only case scheduled. In my opinion, he'd already made his mind up.

And so, the case was adjourned once again. This time, however, I had a growing sense of futility. It seemed that no matter what way I went about trying to get even basic arguments on the record, they would be slapped down as irrelevant, or I'd be interrupted and my chain of thought disrupted.

To my mind, I was in a different world once inside that courtroom, one far removed from logic, common sense and fairness. How many times would I have to say that there were low tactics and outright lies being deployed before someone would take notice?

The day in front of O'Donoghue was a stark lesson in how the courts operate in possession proceedings, at Circuit Court level anyway. The banks had the deep pockets to hire wordsmiths who knew how to play the game. They had endless resources to get what they wanted and from what I had seen over the past couple of years, they had no shame about deploying any and every dirty trick.

The lay litigants trying to save their homes had no training, no resources, no equity of arms, no fair procedures and no one but themselves. In spite of that, I thought I had been doing quite well up to this point, but I certainly saw the "bit of realism" that day. The rules obviously didn't apply to them – just me.

The adjournment date came along in July and my spirit perked up a little when I saw that it would be Judge Griffin hearing matters again. There were only a few cases listed for this day, mine included, so I attended as normal and waited my turn. When the case numbers were called I heard that the first two on the list would go on for quite a lengthy period of time and it would be well after lunch before I got my turn. I'd no choice but to wait.

I spent a lot of that morning walking around Naas with my friend Brian who had travelled out from Laois to offer support. We had plenty of coffees and chats about the state of the country and generally ranting about all and sundry. Brian had been through the same thing as me – he was about six months further along than me, and I'd sat in court beside him when he needed someone there with him. He was getting a sense of déjà vu.

After lunch we checked back in to see where proceedings were at that point. The first case was still going on! After a half hour, Judge Griffin announced that all other cases listed for the day would have to be adjourned to another date. I rolled my eyes and had a feeling that whenever the next date arrived, once again I'd find myself in front of a different Judge and knowing my luck it would be O'Donoghue again.

Was I psychic?

Before Judge O'Donoghue (24 October 2017)[8]

Yes I was.

I walked into court that morning knowing that I was in for a repeat performance. I'd already seen this Judge in action, unfortunately.

Judge O'Donoghue opened by noting that the case had appeared "about eight times" and was "specially fixed to be disposed of once and for all."

Translation: patience exhausted; clock running.

As he had done back in February, Judge O'Donoghue made it clear that he was pressed for time for some reason.

Finola Martin read the fresh figures, neatly collated and ready to be opened to the court. While she recited, O'Donoghue was already writing notes for the order he intended to make.

I reminded him, as I had done back in February, that the Registrar had previously set aside a day and a half for a full hearing – that Judge Fergus had ordered.

> "There won't be any need to spend a day and a half on this unless there's an extraordinary defence to this."

There were still motions before the court and an affidavit that had never been opened. He didn't look up.

[8] The exchanges in this section are fully verifiable from the DAR transcript: 171024 The Governor and Company of the Bank of Ireland v. David Morrissey

Sorry, the Court that's hearing the matter determines how long the issue should take. Now, what witnesses are you calling? What points are you making?

During the summer I'd had my mortgage accounts **forensically audited**, and the analysis showed significant overcharging by the bank. I added that report to my affidavit with supporting exhibits. I attempted to outline the overcharging evidence.

"Have you got that witness here?" he asked.

"No."

"Then you can't give that evidence."

Strike one more argument from consideration before it's even heard on the record.

He reverted to his checklist – employment, income, "When was your last ***full*** payment?" When I admitted it had been a few years earlier, he offered the sentence meant to sound reasonable while ending the argument:

"You can't continue to live in this apartment and not pay."

I replied that that wasn't the case, that I was paying as much as I could manage each month, had been doing so for years and I could back that up with proofs I had with me. It was not a case of me "not paying."

Again, I tried to raise the earlier judicial contradictions – false affidavits, deliberate omissions of received payments, possible perjury during 2016. Again, he waved them all away.

"They've filed a detailed affidavit, and you've no counter-affidavit."

"I **do** have an affidavit, but you've refused to open it to the court."

At that, Judge O'Donoghue put everything down, sneered, and **demanded I state my entire defence orally**. I said that if he wanted to know my defence it would be a far better use of the court's time for him to read it and then ask me to expand on details. He rolled his eyes.

Then came the line that closed my defence completely:

"We can't go on forever and a day on this."

Judge O'Donoghue wanted the case finished as quickly as possible, and nothing I said or presented was ever going to change that. Funny how you can go from the fairness and integrity of Judges O'Sullivan and Griffin to the contemptuous attitudes of Judges Fergus and O'Donoghue in one swift turn.

It was over. He granted **an order for possession**, imposed a six-month stay, refused costs, and told me, with an air of finality:

"If you're not satisfied, you can appeal to the High Court."

"Oh, I most certainly *will* be appealing it, Judge!"

I felt like exploding and calling him every name under the sun, but I held my tongue.

So that was the day the Bank of Ireland "won" its order – and the day I learned what passes for judgment in a possession list: an unread affidavit dismissed as *waffle and nonsense*; a defendant effectively unheard; law firms funded by deep pockets omitting evidence; court instructions ignored; Judges rubber-stamping possession orders while overlooking every procedural defect and low tactic deployed against vulnerable people.

Some might say that the system is absolutely broken. Others might suggest that it is functioning perfectly.

Make your own mind up, dear reader.

Outcome & Reality

Outcome: Possession granted to the Bank of Ireland – six-month stay – no costs.

Reality: Every sworn defence ignored. The Judge admitted on record he wouldn't read the evidence because he wasn't interested in "*waffle and nonsense.*" Expediency came first; fairness an afterthought. Unbelievable bias on clear display.

When court adjourned, I packed the same black file that had carried me through two years of courtroom drama and walked out feeling strangely calm. I was just numb after years of listening to, and putting up with, absolute bollocks.

The possession order may have ended the case, but it didn't erase the record. Those DARs and affidavits remain: carved proof of what really happened in an Irish courtroom when **procedure replaced fair procedures**.

By now I had gone two and half years against what I now saw as an absolutely rotten system. One not interested in justice, just expediency. Peoples' lives are not important, getting the result is – by fair means or foul.

In a way I was relieved it was over – at least the Circuit Court side of it all. I needed to get my head into a better place. Besides going through the mental torture of the actual court process, I'd now been fighting in one way or another for the better part of seven years. I was well and truly knackered.

AFTER THE ORDER
(October 2017–February 2018)

When Bank of Ireland finally secured its possession order on **24 October 2017**, my body and mind simply shut down. Seven years of bank battles, negotiations, brush-offs, and relentless filings had drained me completely. I'd had to contend with it all while trying to live something resembling a normal life. I hadn't taken a holiday in over ten years, and my finances – already tight – were even worse after the endless legal costs. I'd spent a small fortune just keeping those cases alive in court.

To anyone who asked, I said I would appeal – and I meant it – I'd already made that intention very clear in court. But Exhaustion can play cruel tricks. In my case, it did. Somewhere along the line, I convinced myself that the appeal window was **three months**. In reality it was **ten days**.

Whatever way my head worked back then, I remember feeling hollow rather than angry. The paperwork was supposedly over; all I wanted was to take a break. There was a six-month stay on the possession order, so I gave myself what felt like a short break – a few weeks to recover before preparing the appeal. I didn't realise until the end of November that the clock had already run out.

When that hit me, I was dismayed. Even after everything I'd survived in court, I had managed to walk straight into a procedural trap. There was no one else to blame – it was entirely on me. That's why I've said before, and will say again, that none of this book is a manual. Even at that stage, seasoned by hearings and transcripts, I was still capable of getting it wrong, and this one was a serious miss.

With the normal appeal route closed due to me taking my eye off the ball, the only remaining path I could see was a **judicial review** under Article 34 of the Constitution. Surely, I thought, the High Court would see the lack of fair procedures and the bias that had run unchecked in Naas.

Surely it would.

APPEAL AND AFTERMATH
(2018–2021)

Judicial Review before Judge Noonan (February 2018)

By the turn of the year, my earlier resignation had hardened into resolve once more. I spent Christmas drafting, citing every statute and rule I could find. The application was ready before January was over. A few weeks later, in the **Four Courts**, it was finally heard.

This judicial review wasn't a stunt; it was the only mechanism left after the possession order and me messing up on the appeal timeframe – a last attempt to make the High Court examine what the Circuit Court had simply rubber-stamped.

The affidavit I swore that January 2018 laid it all out – bias, refusal of natural justice, perjury in the affidavits of service, omission of payments, refusing to follow court instructions, and the bank's continued failure to prove ownership. It ran to fifteen pages with numbered paragraphs and exhibits, every line drawn from statute or rule. For the first time everything stood in order: clear, correct, complete.

The hearing took place in **Court No. 6** of the Four Courts, the regular Judicial Review list. **Mr. Justice**

Noonan appeared courteous but brisk; to him this was just another file in a long queue. He didn't invite submissions or ask a single question. He simply opened the affidavit, read it silently for a few minutes, then looked down to his bench recorder and began dictating judgment.

It wasn't a dialogue. He spoke quickly – phrases such as "no arguable ground," "within the discretion of the Circuit Court," and "delay fatal to relief." Each line sounded pre-written, as if the conclusion existed before my case was ever filed.

When he finished, he closed the folder, raised his head, and said evenly:

"Accordingly, the application for leave is refused."

That was it. No clarification, no questions, no further comment. He recorded the decision for the official note and moved straight on to the next matter.

I never received, nor ever saw, a written version of the judgment; whatever justification he dictated that afternoon disappeared quietly into the anonymised digital archive, like thousands before it.

Walking out through the long corridors of the Four Courts, I wasn't angry so much as emptied out. Seven years of argument had been distilled into a ten minute refusal. A procedure meant to test fairness had performed its own small imitation of it.

It all appeared that there was nothing left to appeal. The only place remaining within reach was now procedural –

the **Master of the High Court**, keeper of motions, costs, and execution. If Judges no longer wanted the argument, perhaps the paperwork still might.

The next stage would start there.

Before the Master of the High Court (April/May 2018)

The motion before the Master was listed that April. After the stillness of the Judicial Review, the Master's Court felt like another planet – smaller, louder, human. No wigs, no marble solemnity, just a crowded room with files piled high and the sharp crack of the Master's voice above it all.

I had sat in earlier that week to watch how he worked. He didn't tolerate bluff; he interrupted freely and roasted any solicitor or junior counsel who tried it. People whispered his name with the caution you reserve for a dangerous friend – **Edmund Honohan**. To me he looked like the first real sign of integrity I'd seen in a courtroom for years.

When my day came, I discovered I'd made a rookie mistake – not enough copies of my affidavit. The Master wasn't pleased. He fixed me with a frown but let me read the text aloud instead of striking the motion out. **Finola Martin BL**, still acting for the Bank of Ireland, jumped up to object. Mr. Honohan cut her off before she finished her first sentence and told her to sit down.

Then he turned back to me:

"Let's leave this for a week. Come in again next week and bring proper copies," he said, "and I'll read it properly."

That alone felt revolutionary – a Judge figure actually agreeing to read, especially after the way I'd been treated in the Circuit Court a few months earlier.

While we were waiting to be heard, Finola leaned over and said she had to pop out to deal with another case. If ours was called while she was out of the room, would I kindly tell the Master and ask for it to be put back?

"Sure," I said. "Why don't I argue against myself as well if you don't make it back?" I didn't *actually* tell her to sit and swivel, but…

I returned the following week better prepared, three copies in hand. He opened the affidavit himself, asking questions, and pushing me on points of law and procedure. He gave me no special treatment – nor was a seeking any; he simply made sure I was heard. I faltered several times during questioning. He was testing me on clear points of law and finding out if I actually knew what I was talking about or just quoting without understanding. There was no easy ride through his court.

Finally, after reading my affidavit and listening to my arguments, he leaned back and said, almost to himself:

> "This looks like a scenario where the defendant was not allowed to participate… a sorry excuse of a case from start to finish… a clear example of a lay litigant not being heard and not being allowed to offer any defence."

For a moment the courtroom went silent. Then, in measured words, he granted my **application for an extension of time to lodge an appeal – three weeks beyond the date of his order.**

Finola Martin sprang up instantly.

"The plaintiff will be appealing that judgment," she announced.

The Master exploded.

"That is a DISGRACEFUL decision!" he roared.

He had understood what few others had – that the plaintiff's team had already drafted their appeal notice before the hearing even began.

"Don't waste this court's time pretending to listen when your response has been decided in advance!"

He said that he would be contacting Whitney Moore Solicitors personally concerning their behaviour and told Ms. Martin to get out and never appear before him again. His voice echoed all the way to the door.

Honestly, I didn't hide my amusement. Years of being talked over had found a counterweight in three minutes of straight talk from the bench. Before leaving I turned back and said, "Sir, thank you for listening to me." He didn't reply – just kept scribbling – but he heard me.

Outside in the corridor I burst into tears. These weren't tears of sadness, just years of pent-up frustration finally let go. Someone had finally listened. The pressure valve had opened at last. Mr. Honohan had given me a hard time only where it mattered – law and procedure. There was no indulgence, no pity, just fairness. And that single experience proved how a court could and should operate.

If the Circuit Court had worked like that, maybe the result would have been the same – but at least it would have been reached honestly.

I don't know whether Mr. Honohan did actually send that letter chewing out Whitney Moore – I'd like to think he did.

It was around the same time that I was in the Master's Court, that I received a phone call from the Sheriff telling me that he was about to execute the possession order, as instructed by the courts. He asked how long I required to pack up and go and hand him the keys. I stopped him there and asked who had given him his instructions. He declined to name anyone, so I told him that before he came anywhere near my home, he should know that the case was currently in the Master's Court – in other words, it was still active. Executing any possession order on that basis was premature and entirely inappropriate. And if he had not been told this, he had been lied to, so I advised him to seek clarity on the matter before he made a mistake.

Upon hearing this revelation his tone shifted slightly and I could detect a definite note of annoyance – not with me – with whomever had put pressure on him to execute the order. Even though he didn't confirm who it was, I told him *I* knew who it was and he should phone them and give them both barrels. I also told him I would send him written proof that the case was still being heard by posting off copies of the filed affidavits the Master would soon be hearing.

After the conclusion of the listing in the Master's court, I sent the Sheriff a copy of the Master's decision.

I never heard from the Sheriff again.

Before Justice MacGrath (Plaintiff's Appeal 2018–2019)

As soon as the Master granted me the extension, I filed a **Notice of Appeal** in the High Court Central Office. I expected Whitney Moore to move quickly – and they did. Their own appeal against the Master's decision arrived almost immediately, clearly drafted long *before* he had ruled. The very next day after my filing, their affidavit was on my doorstep. So began **Round Two** of the same procedural marathon: affidavit, reply, counter-affidavit – each heavier than the last.

The skirmishes dragged on for months. There were *mentions* before different Judges, most of which never reached substance.

One day the list was so crowded the Judge warned:

"Anyone whose case will take longer than fifteen minutes, apply for another sitting."

I caught sight of **Brendan Moriarty** –who had now obviously deemed the matter to be interesting (or profitable) enough to warrant a personal appearance – once it reached High Court stage – loitering on the other side of the room with Finola Martin beside him. Over the next few minutes, various legal teams made themselves known to the Judge and agreed that 15 minutes would not be enough time and one by one they filed out of the court. I waited patiently for Bren and Finola to do the same thing. After all, by then **five** separate affidavits were in play. I waited for one of them to step forward and request another date. They stayed silent, hoping to sneak their hearing in there and then and obviously try the same blitzkrieg tactic that had served them well at Circuit Court level. I waited until everyone else had spoken, giving them plenty of opportunity to be honest before the court. Just as the Judge was satisfied that all of the longer cases had been removed and was ready to proceed through the now thinned-out list, I rose.

"One moment please and with respect, Judge, my case has five affidavits to be opened today. There's no way these matters can be dealt with properly in fifteen minutes. I'm surprised the plaintiff's team didn't volunteer that information themselves. These things can't be rushed, especially with five affidavits in the mix."

The Judge agreed and pushed it back for mention a few weeks later. Poor oul' Bren – red-faced, furious and not far short of stamping his feet – bundled his papers into his briefcase and stormed out, with Finola following cautiously behind. I won't pretend I didn't enjoy seeing that.

The case re-surfaced that autumn before being assigned to **Mr. Justice MacGrath**. On the first appearance we waited fifteen minutes in complete silence – the contempt both sides had for each other quite obvious – until the Judge entered. Before he had even sat down, Moriarty casually tossed a huge file across the bench toward me. It hit the table with a dull thud.

I refused to touch it.

"Judge, I assume you saw that," I said. "He's just thrown material at me that I've never seen, and was obviously holding it until the last possible moment. They're trying to ambush me. This is just cynical."

Judge MacGrath looked up. "I saw it, Mr. Morrissey. This matter will stand over. Whatever that file is, it must be served by post and in proper time."

He fixed Moriarty with a glance that didn't need any verbalising. Another adjournment, another near foot-stamping tantrum from Bren, and another small victory. Outside the courtroom, as I headed for the exit, Moriarty tried to speak to me and pushed the file towards me again.

I brushed him off with a contemptuous, "don't you fucking speak to me and keep your shit to yourself!" and kept walking.

I need to reiterate once more, this was **not** my appeal against the 2017 possession order that was being decided. It was *Bank of Ireland's* appeal against the Master's judgment. To show how ludicrous the situation had become… they were appealing my right to appeal against the judgment they had been given, where I made my intention to appeal known to the court. Is it any wonder that an ordinary person gets a headache when trying to deal with this shit?

Eventually, on **the last working day before Christmas 2018**, the hearing went ahead. Every affidavit and exhibit lay before the court; the arguments already locked in. Judge MacGrath seemed to read everything, asked a few clarifying questions, but gave nothing away. He said judgment would be reserved for the new year.

Five months later we were recalled for the result.

Justice MacGrath's Judgment (15 May 2019)

For this section, I must first apologise if there is an abundance of legal jargon set out below. A lot of what you will read comes directly from Justice MacGrath's judgment. I've tried to steer clear of legalese throughout this book but paraphrasing a judgment is not a good idea. So please, bear with it – it'll be over soon ;-)

In a calm, almost conversational tone, Judge MacGrath summarised the history: the possession order of **24 October 2017**, my out-of-time appeal, my application before the Master (who had granted me three extra weeks), and Whitney Moore's immediate appeal of that extension. He noted – accurately – that **Judge Noonan** had already refused my judicial review in January 2018.

Every affidavit was recited in sequence: mine, their reply from **Helen Dorris**, my rejoinder, Moriarty's, and the final exchange that summer. He acknowledged that the Master had described the Circuit Court proceedings as *"a sorry excuse of a case from start to finish."*

But he made clear that his court would be confined to legal principle, not sympathy.

The Bank's case: I had consciously chosen judicial review instead of appeal; therefore no "operative mistake." They leaned on *ACC v Fagan* – where a borrower who did the same lost – and argued that my application was barred both by precedent and by *Henderson v Henderson* (no re-litigation of decided issues).

My case: I had intended to appeal but, exhausted, misread the rule; I had no legal advice; the Master exercised discretion fairly because the original hearing denied me participation and the delay caused no prejudice. I argued that *Fagan* was distinguishable: there the borrower's case had been heard on its merits – mine never had.

Judge MacGrath accepted one part: that I had genuinely *formed* an intention to appeal within ten days. But he drew the line there. Relying on *Éire Continental Trading v Clonmel Foods Ltd*, *Brewer v Commissioners of Public Works*, and *Goode Concrete v CRH plc*, he recited the classic three-part test:

- Bona fide intention to appeal;
- An operative mistake; and
- An arguable ground of appeal.

He found that while the first limb was met, the second was not. Citing *Fagan*, he held that choosing judicial review over appeal was a **"deliberate and conscious decision,"** not a mistake. Ignorance of the ten-day rule, even if genuine, was not "operative." Everything I alleged – bias, denial of documents, exclusion – had been known to me on the day of the Circuit hearing; no new facts justified discretion under *Goode Concrete.*

In conclusion he wrote – and read in open court:

"I am not satisfied that a mistake occurred as that term is understood...All of the material facts upon which Mr. Morrissey intends to rely, were before the court. It would not be in accordance with the overall administration of justice and the balance of justice as between the parties to permit the appeal to proceed. I must therefore allow the plaintiff's appeal."

And just like that, **the Master's decision was overturned.**

To add what felt like the final kick in the teeth, Judge MacGrath awarded costs to the plaintiff. The figure I now supposedly owed approached half a million euro – another case of a bank pulling numbers out of its arse. Judge MacGrath asked if I had capacity to pay. I stared at him for a few seconds, stunned, wondering to myself what planet these clowns were living on, then said I'd be happy to donate whichever kidney he preferred – or both, if that's what the court preferred. No sense being polite anymore. He didn't appreciate that comment but I no longer gave an airborne intercourse.

To the Supreme Court (2019–2020)

Once Judge MacGrath's judgment was perfected, Whitney Moore wasted no time demanding voluntary surrender, informing me I had "exhausted all legal means." As far as I was concerned, I hadn't. I wasn't about to be bullied by a smug twat in Ballsbridge into handing over my keys. I had a six month stay past the date of perfection of the order and I didn't appreciate Moriarty acting the prick and kicking me while I was down. Any time they sent another letter, I told them where they could stick it – one of those letters even spelled it out exactly like that. To hell with any decorum or politeness now – they could simply go fuck themselves and I told them as much.

In truth I'd lost all confidence in the legal system long before – probably since the first hearings in Naas – but dragging the machine this far had become its own form of satisfaction. If they were determined to grind me down, I'd continue to make them work every inch of the way for it.

Next stop: **the Supreme Court.**

When Judge MacGrath delivered his decision in May 2019 – perfected that June – I knew the only avenue left was upwards. If discretion and procedure had erased substance, then only the Supreme Court might restore it. That was the plan.

I spent that summer learning how to petition under **Article 34 and Order 58 of the Rules of the Superior Courts**. There was no right of appeal – only the possibility of *leave* to appeal, proving a point of general public importance or that justice required it.

The document, headed *"SUPREME COURT APPEAL: Record No. 2018/78 CA"*, traced the chain clearly: the possession order of 24 October 2017; Noonan's refusal of judicial review; Honohan's extension (April 2018); and MacGrath's reversal (May 2019).

I argued that the case raised identical questions to *Senior Money Mortgages v Gately* and *Pepper Finance v Cannon*: how courts decide extensions of appeal time and whether Ireland's boilerplate mortgage clauses comply with EU consumer protection and data privacy law. I asked the court to treat them as matters of **general public importance** and to refer issues to the **Court of Justice of the European Union**. The appendix listed seventeen grounds of appeal – from denial of fair hearing to incompatibility with European law.

By early 2020 the application was lodged, clocked, and acknowledged. Whitney Moore were personally served in February 2020. Then came the long silence: form letters from the Supreme Court Office every few months – "Under judicial consideration by the President as to admissibility." It felt like waiting for weather to change.

Finally, a thin envelope in late 2020:

"Having considered the application, the Court is not satisfied that any point of general or exceptional public importance arises. Leave to appeal is refused."

Obviously, lay litigants being steam rollered in Irish courts isn't something of public importance. We can't upset that particular apple cart now can we?

No commentary, no reasoning – just one word that travels faster than any judgment: **Refused.**

THE LSRA COMPLAINT AND THE RECORDS

(2020–2021)

After the Supreme Court's refusal in late 2020, I turned from battling the system to holding its practitioners to account. If the courts wouldn't question what had happened inside their own walls, maybe the **Legal Services Regulatory Authority** would.

In **December 2020** I filed a detailed complaint against **Luke Hanahoe**, partner at **Hanahoe & Hanahoe Solicitors in Naas**, who had acted as Whitney Moore's local agent during the early hearings. You may of course remember him as Mr Actingfortheplaintiff.

The complaint set out, date by date, how he had argued for the bank through 2015 and 2016, and how on **10 May 2016** he remained silent when counsel claimed that no payments had been made since 2012 – even though he had personally stood before the court months earlier acknowledging those very payments – on the record.

The exhibits told the story: postal order receipts, bank statements, delivery slips, and two certified **Digital Audio Recording (DAR)** transcripts – one from June 2015 and the other from May 2016 – capturing Judge Griffin's line:

"If this man hadn't turned up and handed me his receipts, I'd have to assume he'd walked away. Which is clearly not the case."

Those recordings became Exhibits A and B of the LSRA complaint.

Getting them had cost me a small fortune. Each Judge from the original circuit retained custody of their own recordings, which meant travelling cross-country to where each Judge was currently sitting for **ex parte applications in Cork, Bray, Galway and Naas** to authorise release for transcription. The Registrar's order was easy – Naas – but one Judge had been reassigned to the **Special Criminal Court**, and he was there another six months before I could re-apply when he returned to the circuit. Between travel, filing fees, and transcription costs, the DARs were the most expensive evidence I'd ever purchased – but they were mine, and they were official.

With that evidence I submitted the formal LSRA Form 20/4442 on 14 December 2020, citing **Chapter 5.1(c)** of the *Solicitors' Guide to Professional Conduct*: "A solicitor should not deceive, or knowingly or recklessly mislead the court."

Hanahoe's first response in January 2021 was everything expected: irrelevant autobiography, talk of workload and memory lapses, and a defence that it was "impossible to remember every nuance" of older cases. He must have never kept proper files.

He also mentioned that he had contacted Whitney Moore for some inexplicable reason, who replied to him saying that they didn't even need to look up my file. I couldn't help noticing that I'd clearly occupied a certain amount of headspace at Whitney Moore. They apparently didn't even need to look up the file to remember me. Hanahoe even added in mentions of dates and events he wasn't even a party to, referencing listings that had happened *after* his involvement, which he had zero first-hand knowledge of – as if they somehow had any relevance to the complaint. They didn't.

It was waffle and back-pedalling on a grand scale.

In April I filed a meticulous rebuttal, referencing DAR timestamps that destroyed each denial. His second submission in May – once again referencing events that happened *after* he had been involved in any capacity – drew another point-by-point reply from me that June. Whatever happened later, I said, the alleged misconduct occurred on 10 May 2016 in Naas Circuit Court – captured verbatim on DAR.

Through the summer the Authority was silent. Then on **24 September 2021** the decision arrived, abrupt and final:

"Having conducted a preliminary review…I determine the complaint to be inadmissible without substance or foundation, as instructions to the barrister did not come from Mr. Hanahoe."

In short: for the purposes of this complaint, I had aimed at the wrong target.

A single sentence erased a year of submissions. A follow-up letter confirmed the Authority would take no further action – no appeal – and hinted that if I was dissatisfied I could approach the Ombudsman, but only about procedure, not conduct.

Reading that, the architecture of blame finally appeared. Hanahoe had spoken in Naas, but the

instructions and affidavits came from **Whitney Moore LLP** – the Bank of Ireland's solicitors in Ballsbridge. Under the LSRA's narrow reading of the Act, liability rested with the instructing solicitor, not the agent who repeated the instruction.

Still, it wasn't wasted. The LSRA file itself – complete with certified transcripts, letters, and the determination form – became an official acknowledgement that the misleading statements of 2016 had been reviewed by a statutorily independent body. While the file remained open, there were no new enforcement motions and no further correspondence. Whether the complaint caused that silence, I cannot know; what it gave me in practice was time.

When the Authority closed the matter in October 2021, I realised the next move couldn't come from a regulator's form – it had to come from the evidence itself. The DARs were the proof. For the first time since 2014 I held in my hands an official record that spoke louder than any affidavit, revealing who gave the instructions, who repeated them, and where the case was really being directed from.

THE ARMISTICE

After the LSRA letter arrived in October 2021, everything went silent. Seven years of litigation, filings, and motions ended not with another judgment but with an administrative shrug. The war paused at that point. I expected something to happen again soon, but it didn't.

Bank of Ireland hadn't retreated, but it hadn't advanced either. Whitney Moore froze; Luke Hanahoe vanished into new cases; and I was no longer being forced to live in legal la-la land. After so many battles in musty courtrooms, the silence felt almost alien, but most welcome.

For the first time since 2014 there were no deadlines, no demands, no dates circled in red. I was still in my apartment, the papers boxed, transcripts stacked in labelled folders. If nothing else, there was breathing space – and the awareness that the story wasn't over. Every pleading, order, and mis-step had been catalogued and I'd pull them out again if and when necessary.

They had the possession order, but it was never successfully executed – despite one single, inappropriate attempt and a few bullying demands that were replied to with a slap. That one execution attempt occurred while I was still holding them up in the High Court, around the time the Master was lambasting Finola Martin BL to my considerable amusement. The sheriff was told legal matters were still ongoing, and at the time of writing, that was the last I heard from him.

Why nothing happened after October 2021 I cannot say. Perhaps the LSRA complaint played a part. Perhaps the outstanding proceedings did. Perhaps it was simply a commercial decision. Whatever the reason, everything stopped.

Maybe they knew I had the DARs. Or maybe I was simply too unpredictable. I had never played by their rules – and that wasn't going to change. As a lay litigant I'm not in any way obliged to genuflect, bow or doff the cap. I believe that irritates the shit out of them– and perhaps even frightens them.

With things quiet for the first time in years, I slipped back into something resembling normal life. I did still have a couple of routes left open if they ever crawled out again, but I'll keep those in reserve.

From October 2021 I switched myself off and got on with my life. I knew things weren't over – they were not going to leave things there when 30 pieces of silver (plus Mickey Mouse, freshly pulled-out-of-the-arse, fictitious fees and interest amounts) and someone's home were still out there to be grasped – but until something else happened I wasn't going to spend any more time worrying about it.

CLANE
(March 2023)

I'm still in my apartment!

AFTERWORD

I don't like bullies.

Nobody really does, but if you think bullies are just stereotypical schoolyard tough guys, you need to look a bit wider.

My first real encounter with a typical bully was, like most others, a gobshite in school who thought he was untouchable. During some classes he sat in front of me and liked turning around to land a cheap hit when the teacher's back was turned. He wasn't tough – just loud, lazy, and a bit of a thick shit who was held back a year *because* he was a thick shit. His hilarious antics went on for a few weeks until he tried it once too often and my fist met his face.

Naturally, this time the teacher caught it, and we were both dispatched to the headmaster's office. I explained what had been happening and the headmaster believed me, because as it turned out, this wasn't the first time tough guy had been reported for being a dickhead. I was sent home for the day; he was suspended for two weeks, and when he came back, the swagger was gone. If we passed each other in the corridor, I made sure to look him squarely in the eye each time. Strangely, he never tried any tough guy antics again.

That lesson stayed with me: a bully of any sort keeps going until you make him stop. Once you do, he usually folds faster than you expect.

The grown-up world has its bullies too. They wear suits instead of school jumpers and hide behind headed paper. They don't need muscle when threats typed in legal language will do. They use fear the way a craftsperson uses tools – cleanly, without conscience, and always for pay. They call it "advocacy." I call it Small Mickey Syndrome with a law degree.

They can lie by omission, mislead by phrasing, and still sleep soundly, because the culture rewards winning, not honour. If you catch them out, they act shocked that anyone dared talk back. Respect is demanded, but never earned.

Once I had lost the initial fear, replying to their letters became almost enjoyable. They never expected sarcasm in return envelopes or reasoned challenges coming from someone without a degree. So I took great pleasure in foregoing the legalese and composing some home truths in plain English. Some of those letters were even used as exhibits against me, much to my amusement. They can dish it out but they cry to the judge when their intended victim throws it back in their face.

sob "Mr. Morrissey is being nasty to us, Judge!" **sob** Aw diddums!

The truth is that bullies haven't disappeared since childhood – they've simply gone professional. They run offices, sit on boards, and uphold systems that rely on fear to function. And they lose their power the instant you lose the fear.

So lose the fear!

I have always lived my life by one simple rule:
Do no harm… but take no shit.

WITHOUT PREJUDICE

PART TWO

...BUT TAKE NO SHIT!

PREVIEW

HERE WE GO AGAIN!

As I write this, it's late July 2026, and I have already been back in the Circuit Court four times this year. What I discovered in late 2025 was that the old case had somehow come back to life under the same record number: 2014/EJ331. Court appearances had taken place during 2025 without my knowledge or participation, and I knew absolutely nothing about any of it until the morning of another scheduled listing.

How did I actually find out?

At 10:15am on 21 November 2025, I received a WhatsApp message from a third party wishing me good luck in court. Good luck in court? That was news to me. For roughly five years I had received no communication from any law firm, no court papers, no service of documents and no indication whatsoever that anything was happening. And suddenly, by sheer chance I find out that my name is on a court listing that very afternoon?

So the circus, apparently, had started up all over again.

I raced into Naas Circuit Court, writing off a day's much-needed work in the process, and discovered that a firm I had never previously dealt with was appearing in connection with an application involving a new party. At the same time, the court list continued to identify Bank of Ireland and Whitney Moore in connection with the matter.

The second the case was called, I made my objections rather forcefully. In fact, any residual courtroom diplomacy I might once have possessed went right out the window. I discovered there and then – and *only* there and then – that substantive orders were apparently being sought in proceedings I had not even known were active. Had I not received that WhatsApp message and made it into court, I would not have been there to object at all.

The Registrar appeared visibly annoyed and adjourned the matter. I left that courtroom absolutely fucking furious and immediately made a complaint to the Legal Services Regulatory Authority.
At that point I did not yet know the full history of what had happened during 2025, so I started digging.

What I subsequently discovered was that the old record number had **already** been listed before the court *several times* that year **without my knowledge**. I also discovered issues concerning which solicitors were formally on record at various stages and when notices relating to representation were actually filed and served. Those matters now form part of the documentary trail behind Part Two.

Over the following months I gradually pieced together the sequence of events from court records, correspondence and filings. Some of what I found was familiar. Far too bloody familiar, in fact. The same questions began appearing again: who knew what, who was formally on record, what had been put before the court, what had happened while I wasn't there, and why had nobody thought it good manners to tell me?

Naturally, I wanted the Digital Audio Recordings of the 2025 appearances. Those recordings would show exactly what had been said in court in my absence and might also have been relevant to issues raised in my continuing complaint to the LSRA. So I applied to obtain them.

It took four trips into court and six months to actually get the DAR Motion heard. The application was refused.

I disagreed fundamentally with that decision and with the suggestion that the recordings were unnecessary for the purposes of fair procedures. Whatever else might be said about them, the DARs were the only verbatim record of hearings at which I had not been present. How in the hell was I supposed to properly deal with proceedings when I wasn't even allowed to know what had been said in my absence? Sound familiar? I thought so too.

Fair procedures, my arse!

And that's where things currently stand because the story is not finished. The proceedings are ongoing, the regulatory issues are ongoing, more documents are appearing, more hearings are taking place and Part Two is being written as events unfold.

What I *can* say is that I am already dozens of pages into it. When the dust finally settles – whatever the outcome – ***Without Prejudice: Part Two*** will document what happened, what was said, what the records show, and what individuals were involved. As before, the paperwork will speak for itself.

It may take a while. But it's coming.

Again, I wish you well.

David Morrissey
25 July 2026

ACKNOWLEDGEMENTS

No one fights alone – not really. I wouldn't have got through the last sixteen-odd years without help.

Going up against banks, obscenely paid legal firms, and what seems to be the entire court system itself is a long, lonely road that appears to have no end in sight – but I have more people on my side now than I did when this all started and I have a lot more knowledge to draw upon.

My gratitude must go firstly to Byron and Adrienne from *The Hub Ireland*. They are in a similar situation to myself but they've never stopped fighting the good fight and share their experience and knowledge with all those who need it, myself included. When I needed a pep talk they were always on hand; when I couldn't wrap my head around the endless legal procedures, they had documents that helped make sense of it all; and when I came out of court they were there to help me understand what had happened and where to go next. They never gave legal advice, they just made sense of it all. I have no doubt whatsoever that I'd have been out on my ear years ago if not for them. They've never made money from helping people out, relying purely on donations, but I definitely think they've saved many people's lives and homes and wish them all the very best in their own continuing battles. Byron reely needz 2 start useing his spelll chekker dough ;-).

Brian Smyth, Sharon Williams and Rachel O'Brien were there with me in the courtrooms numerous times over that 2015–2020 period. One of them was always there, and that meant more than I can adequately express. Although there was nothing they could do to help me argue my case on those days, just my knowing that someone was there with me in those horrible rooms made things feel a lot less solitary. They also took many contemporaneous notes while I was on my feet trying to get blood from various stones, which helped fill in the blanks when I was compiling a summary of that day's events. I'd have lost a lot of important information to posterity if they hadn't been writing it all down as it happened.

Simon Goldberg's *White Rabbit Trust* videos were essential viewing for me over the last ten to fifteen years. Simon is a former UK banker who has returned from the dark side to share his extensive experience in the industry. His videos were both informative and hilarious, especially the ones where he phoned companies as he was recording and exposed their shithousery in real time. Highly recommended. He's someone who doesn't take kindly to people trying to make money from the misfortunes of others, has no patience for fraud or deceit and calls it as it is… we need more like him. I've never met Simon but I'll happily buy him a pint if I do.

Vin Byrne's Sunday evening broadcasts on TNS radio were always interesting and I rarely missed them. Vin spoke on a variety of matters relating to common law, contracts and personal power and I learned a lot of valuable information from his shows. They were bloody good for keeping my morale up too. Vin got me thinking in different ways, and I credit him with furthering my understanding of contract law. I'd never have heard of the 'Official Offer' without him. That *Official Offer* was crucial in my defence

– even as the solicitors and barristers on the other side tried hard to omit it from their affidavits.

Kudos must also go to the ordinary men and women I crossed paths with during the early part of this journey: *Irish Homeowners Unite*, *The Defend Our Homes League*, *The Peoples' Association Watchdog* and *The Anti-Eviction Taskforce*. Our association may have been relatively brief, but it was from meeting you and talking to you that I learned that there were many other people with the same concerns and problems that I had. We weren't alone. Your principles were honest, your motives noble. My admiration for you all remains. I hope to see you all again in the future.

My family members probably all thought I'd gone barmy when it all kicked off, especially with some of the stories I was telling them about what was going on. I've no doubt they didn't believe what they were hearing, but I like to think that the longer it all went on and the more determined I got, the more they began to believe I was doing something right. So thanks for hanging in there. Seems the mad brother isn't so mad after all.

I'd also like to thank everyone of a legal persuasion. You gave me an education I never expected to receive, even if it wasn't the one you intended to provide. Similarly, all those public representatives who changed the legislation to bring *'comfort and clarity to the banks'* and rushed to close off any avenues that were previously open whenever the small guy had anything close to a victory. In my opinion, you showed your true colours there folks.

I must, however, give genuine acknowledgement to Edmund Honohan, the Master of the High Court, who in all my years of being in courtrooms, showed himself to be the only legally trained person I ever appeared before who was intent on making sure everything was done correctly and according to fair procedures. He remains the sole individual from that first case who actually listened to my defence. If there were more Edmund Honohans, the legal system might not be the cesspit I've witnessed first-hand. Debt cases were subsequently removed from his court. Whether his predilection toward proper procedure, law and fairness had anything to do with that is not for me to say, although I found it telling.

I'd like to acknowledge all those on the interweb who gave me quite a roller coaster ride. Not just those who provided me with usable knowledge, but also those chancers who showed me that you shouldn't believe everything you see on the net. There is an awful lot of absolute tripe online and I got better at spotting it as time went on. If someone can't answer basic questions or provide tangible proof of success then it's time to call horseshit and move along.

Finally, to all those who find themselves battling soulless legal entities while trying to hang onto their homes... I know what you're going through. I've met some of you. I've been there. But **never** feel ashamed of the position you are in. **Never** retreat into yourselves and **never** believe you are isolated. There are **always** people you can reach out to and talk to.

You are never alone, even when the machinery around you makes you feel that way.

ABOUT THE AUTHOR

David Morrissey is not a lawyer. He has no legal qualifications and no desire to ever set foot in a courtroom again once this is all over. What he does have is sixteen years of experience being dragged through the Irish legal system, and a stubborn refusal to be intimidated by headed paper.

By day, he's a graphic designer. By night – or whenever the gig demands it – he plays guitar in a band called *Celtic Legacy*, which has been making noise for nearly thirty years. He shares his home in Clane, Co. Kildare with an adopted Border Collie and a partner who has supported him every step of the way. He was raised with manners, and the Irish legal system has not managed to knock them out of him yet.

He bought his apartment in 1999 and lived an ordinary life until the crash of 2008 upended everything. What followed was a slow-motion education in how the courts really work.

Without Prejudice: Part One is his first book. No prizes for guessing what his second one will be.

He still lives in Clane. He still designs for a living. He still plays in the band.

And he still takes no shit from solicitors.

PRIVATE AND CONFIDENTIAL
Whitney Moore Solicitors
Wilton Park House
Wilton Place
Dublin 2

25th September 2015

Ref: EJ331/14 and your continuing obfuscation & refusal to sod off

---

FAO: *'WhitneyMoore' that non-existent, mystical non-living entity that seems to have the inexplicable, obviously magical ability to sign documents in a variety of different styles from letter to letter and mistakenly thinks it has some kind of power of authority and/or misguided sense of superiority over a living, breathing, flesh & blood man.*
CC: *Everyone else in Wilton Park House who is actually alive and draws breath.*

Dear Interloper that's obviously hard of hearing,

'DON'T CONTACT ME AGAIN!' was visible very clearly in my last reply to you. What part of that easily understood, four-word statement are you having difficulty with? Is your eyesight failing or do you all have a collective blind spot when it comes to writing and indeed comprehending simple, plain language? Three of the words consisted of 5 letters or less and only two of them had more than one syllable. Now even children of junior infant grade can grasp that level of basic reading and writing. I guess it's a struggle for solicitors and it seems to be a common problem.

To help you out, here it is again in a selection of fonts made a lot bigger and in regular, italicised and bold versions - just in case your myopia, arrogance or simple-mindedness prevents you seeing one, or all instances of them properly. In case of any possible inability to recognise the colour black, I've also made a multi-coloured one too, which, even if you can't see things in black & white, should leap out at you from the page in all its multi-coloured splendour.

DON'T CONTACT ME AGAIN!

DON'T CONTACT ME AGAIN!

DON'T CONTACT ME AGAIN!

DON'T CONTACT ME AGAIN!

DON'T CONTACT ME AGAIN!

You must admit that's very considerate of me. I trust that now leaves no room for any misunderstanding. But if you still cannot grasp the message, please seek the professional guidance of either an optician, a primary school teacher or a counsellor. Doing some yoga or daily meditations might help you belatedly get in touch with your basic humanity, although I suspect you're already too far gone to be saved.

I have no intention of responding to your farcical claims in that last unwanted letter of 23rd September 2015, as it is now clear that you are simply not interested in presenting or using facts and truths – merely distorting them, OR as you've already demonstrated on June 22nd 2015, attempting to conceal them, (in a Courtroom, that's called 'Perjury' … be VERY careful). I am very much looking forward to seeing how you attempt to spin it in Court on October 12th 2015.

You should also realise by now that your constant, pathetic attempts to intimidate me by strategically reminding me of your intention to go for 'Final Orders' on October 12th do nothing except show you up for the cowards you are. I see you've again chickened out of signing a real name to the latest unwanted letter you sent. Cowardly habits are obviously ingrained deeply among arrogant gobshites … no offence, just an observation.

And just in case your memory capacity is akin to that of a goldfish, here's a reminder of something that was on the previous page:

DON'T CONTACT ME AGAIN!

Now sod off!

Sincerely, without ill-will or vexation,

David Morrissey

WITHOUT PREJUDICE

INSIDE AN IRISH COURTROOM AND THE ILLUSION OF FAIRNESS

PART ONE

www.ingramcontent.com/pod-product-compliance
Lightning Source LLC
LaVergne TN
LVHW100158061126
851857LV00010B/306